Marxism in the Pan-African Struggle

Restoring the African Mind
Research Collection

1 THE NEO-COLONIAL CLASS IN POWER

In a lecture titled "Crisis in the Periphery: Africa and the Caribbean," Walter Rodney spoke at length about some of the challenges which confronted post-colonial societies in Africa and the Caribbean. Not only did he speak about the reactionary leadership which took power and maintained the prior colonial system, but he also spoke about the challenge of developing a proper ideological approach to addressing this crisis in post-colonial societies.

African and Caribbean societies were emerging into independence out of the trauma and the hardships of the colonial period. This period also witnessed the emergence of a particular type of leadership which perpetuated the brutality and the viciousness of the prior colonial system. Julius Nyerere, the first president of Tanzania, stated of these elites: "In practice, colonialism, with its implications of racial superiority, was replaced by a combination of neo-colonialism and government by local elites who too often had learned to despise their own African traditions and the mass of the people who worked on the land. External control of African economies continued, usually by the former colonial power."

There was a very deliberate effort to get the elites to despite their own traditions. Education within colonial societies were designed especially to instill this cultural alienation. Education in Africa was organized in a system of age grades, and what one learned was directly linked to which level of the age grade one belonged to. Children learned the basic necessities needed to deal with the challenges of society; which included being able to name certain plants and animals. As they grew older, they were given more specialized knowledge. This education was not only divided on age, but also on gender, thus young girls got a type of education that would prepare them for woman-hood. They were trained in childcare, cooking, social relations, and how to be successful wives and maintain an intimate relationship with their husbands.

We find that within African societies boys were educated in preparation for manhood and girls were educated in preparation for womanhood. This education was done through initiation societies. In Sierra Leone and Liberia, for example, there was the Poro society for boys and the Sande society for girls, which prepared boys and girls for adulthood. In *The Dark Child* (1945), Camara Laye describes the experience of being initiated in the bush schools of Guinea, stating: "The teaching we received in the bush, far from all prying eyes, had nothing very mysterious about it; nothing, I think, that was not fit for ears other than our own. These lessons, the same as had been taught to all who had preceded us, confined themselves to outlining what a man's conduct should be: we were to be absolutely straightforward, to cultivate all the virtues that go to make an honest man, to fulfill our duties toward God, toward our parents, our superiors and our neighbors. We must tell nothing of what we learned, either to women or to the uninitiated; neither were we to reveal any of the secret rites or circumcision. That is the custom. Women, too, are not allowed to tell anything about the rites of excision."

The communal and holistic nature of education in African societies provides African children with advantages that children in Western societies do not demonstrate. Marcelle Geber noticed this when she tested three hundred babies in Uganda. She found that the infants there were superior to Western children when it came to psychological maturity, coordination, and language skills. Interestingly, Geber found that children of more educated parents were less mature than the babies of mothers that were uneducated. The key difference was that the uneducated mother had a stronger attachment to the child. Therefore, it is the family orientated and communal elements of traditional African society that contributed to the development of children to the point that they matured quicker than children living in more developed countries in the Western world. This communal approach to education differs greatly with the more individual approach of Western education. The education which the colonial powers introduced reinforced the cultural values of the colonial powers. This was the education which the neo-colonial elites received.

Of course, the neo-colonial elites were motivated

by more than just their colonial training. They also wanted to replace the colonizers as the exploiters of the masses so that they could accumulate wealth. By the time that Jospeh Mobutu was overthrown in Zaire, he was one of the richest men in the world, having an estimated $4 billion. He owned a yacht, a private jet, and homes in various European countries.

Rodney spoke of the situation in Uganda, where someone like Idi Amin who was both a buffoon and a murderer could be the president of the country. This was the sort of situation which was seen throughout the post-colonial world to varying degrees. Political leaders could be incompetent and ineffective buffoons with an unsatiable desire for adulation, which was often taken to laughably absurd levels, yet those same leaders also often engaged in the murder and torture of their own population.

Amin was also a very typical example of the nature of the neo-colonial elite in power. Amin was not formally educated by the colonial powers, but he was trained by them nevertheless. Amin was recruited to serve in the King's African Rifles in Kenya. Amin was barely literate, but he was someone with a large physique and great athletic ability. He was the national heavyweight boxing champion for several years. He was able to win the favor of British officers due to his loyalty and the role he played in helping to brutally suppress the Mau Mau rebellion in Kenya. Amin eventually rose to the rank of sergeant major, which was the highest position available to an African in the colonial army. Amin became the president of Uganda in 1971 after a coup which overthrew Milton Obote. The British opted to recognize Amin's government and provided support for him, but the relationship between Amin and Britain became strained over time due to Amin's uncontrollable and unpredictable behavior.

In Togo under Gnassingbé Eyadéma, citizens were made to line up to clap for him four times during the day, including when he was on his lunch break. Those who were caught not clapping for him were arrested. Civil servants were also made to wear uniforms with his image on it and to dance for him. The absurdity of this would almost be humorous if not for the tortures and killings which the Togolese people had to endure simply to appease the ego of Eyadéma. Eyadéma, like Amin, was a colonial soldier before seizing power.

Leon M'ba, who was the president of Gabon, was known to have said that all Gabonese have two fatherlands, Gabon and France. A *New York Times* report from 1964 described M'ba, who had recently been overthrown, as "one of France's best friends in Africa." This is type of deep-seated attachment to colonialism which the neo-colonial powers displayed.

One of the most brutal and tragic examples we can look at is the state of the Central African Republic under the dictatorship of Jean-Bedel Bokassa. Bokassa was a child when his father was beaten to death by a French colonial officer for protesting the forced labor policies in the colony. Shortly after the death of his father, Bokassa's mother committed suicide out of grief. In this regard, Bokassa's upbringing was marked by the brutality and violence of French colonialism in Africa. Therefore, it is little wonder why Bokassa himself grew to become such a vicious and violent man.

Despite the fact that it was a French colonial officer that brutally killed his father and that France had oppressed his nation, Bokassa was a loyal servant of France. He fought in the French army during World War II. Bokassa left the army in 1961 and helped to establish a national army in the Central African Republic. Bokassa overthrew his own cousin, David Dacko, in 1965. Bokassa, who cultivated a cult of personality around himself, used government funds to enrich himself. Bokassa held a number of properties in Europe, including a fifty-room mansion in France. While Bokassa was enriching himself from his position, the Central African Republic remained a poor, suffering, and underdeveloped nation.

The excesses of Bokassa's regime were supported by France. It was France that helped to pay for Bokassa's coronation as emperor of the Central African Republic in 1977. Altogether, the coronation cost $22 million—money which was desperately needed in a nation with high infant mortality, widespread illiteracy, and few paved roads. Bokassa later stated that France paying for the coronation was the least they could do to repay him for his services as a soldier who fought for France. Not only was France supplying material support for Bokassa's regime, but Bokassa saw France as an inspiration for his rule. Bokassa was inspired by the example of Napoleon, whom Bokassa described as a "guide and inspiration." Bokassa was also very fond of Charles de Gaulle, whom he referred to as "Papa."

Independence for these colonial societies coincided with the Cold War, which was a struggle between the United States and the Soviet Union. One of the main features of this struggle was the ideological clash between the capitalism of the United States and the socialism of the Soviet Union. As African and

Caribbean countries gained independence, they were also wrestling with whether to adopt capitalism or Marxism. This same question was also confronting Africans in the United States, who were beginning to question the entire capitalistic structure of the United States and who were paying close attention to the Marxist revolutions which were being carried out in other parts of the world, particularly in Cuba and in China.

These critical views of capitalism were expressed by Malcolm X who was taking an interest in the socialist projects which he noticed were taking placed in the colonized world. Malcolm explained: "I've had an opportunity to do a lot of it in the Middle East and Africa. While I was traveling I noticed that most of the countries that had recently emerged into independence have turned away from the so-called capitalistic system in the direction of socialism. So out of curiosity, I can't resist the temptation to do a little investigating wherever that particular philosophy happens to be in existence or an attempt is being made to bring it into existence."

Countries which were coming out of colonialism were rejecting colonialism and the capitalist economic system which sustained colonialism. These nations also looked to nations which had launched successful revolutions such as Russia and China. There was Cuba as well. Marcus Garvey never became a socialist, but he recognized the importance of the Russian Revolution in 1917. In the 1960s, Malcolm was also coming to recognize the significance of the socialist anti-colonial struggles which were being waged around the world.

Malcolm had never reached a point where he fully

embraced socialism. When questioned on which economic system he wanted, Malcolm stated that he did not know, but he was flexible. He also added: "It's impossible for a white person to believe in capitalism and not believe in racism. You can't have capitalism without racism. And if you find one and you happen to get that person into a conversation and they have a philosophy that makes you sure they don't have this racism in their outlook, usually they're socialists or their political philosophy is socialism." Based on Malcolm's response, it seemed that Malcolm was critical of capitalism, but he also was not ready to fully embrace socialism as a solution.

One of the problems that Africans ran into was that white socialists still retained some of the racist attitudes of the dominant society. Assata Shakur explained that she began thinking of herself as a socialist, but she could not join any of the socialist groups which she came into contact with. She explained that she could not "stand the condescending, paternalistic attitudes of some of the white people in those groups." She also explained that she "couldn't relate to the idea of the great white father on earth any more than [I] could relate to the great white father up in the sky."

Africans who were engaged in the socialist struggle against capitalism had to confront the fact that the theories of Karl Marx were developed in Europe by a European man. This created the feeling that, as Shakur explained, Europeans "had a monopoly on Marx and acted like the only experts in the world on socialism came from Europe." For this reason, it was important for African socialists to be able to look to Third World revolutionary leaders who had embraced socialism. Shakur gave the examples of Fidel Castro, Ho Chi Minh, and Agostinho Neto as Third World revolutionaries who made contributions to the revolutionary socialist movement. Mao Tse-tung of China was another such individual.

Mao represented a non-white revolutionary who engaged in a successful revolution. Not only did this demonstrate that Europeans did not have a monopoly on Marxism, but it also created a sense of global solidarity among the non-white peoples of the world.

The Bandung Conference, which was held in 1955, was a conference which was attended by African and Asian nations. Malcolm spoke about this conference in his "Ballot or the Bullet" speech. Malcolm explained that those who attended the conference had differences, such as religious differences. Despite this, the thing that united them was that they were not white. Malcolm explained: "The number-one thing that was not allowed to attend the Bandung conference was the white man. He couldn't come. Once they excluded the white man, they found that they could get together. Once they kept him out, everybody else fell right in and fell in line." Malcolm also explained: "They realized all over the world where the dark man was being oppressed, he was being oppressed by the white man; where the dark man was being exploited, he was being exploited by the white man. So they got together on this basis—that they had a common enemy."

Malcolm expressed the view that whenever white people were engaged in a revolution, that revolution was fought on the basis of white nationalism. Malcolm explained: "The American Revolution was white nationalism. The French Revolution was white nationalism. The Russian Revolution too — yes, it was — white nationalism. You don't think so? Why do you think Khrushchev and Mao can't get their heads together? White nationalism." Here Malcolm was expressing the view that whenever white people engaged in a revolution, it was done on the basis of asserting white interests and that Russia was no different.

In an interview with Robert Penn, Malcolm pointed out that he preferred Mao's approach over the more passive approach of Jawaharlal Nehru, who was India's first prime minister. Malcolm explained: "I think that Nehru brought his country up in a beggar's role. Their roles, the role of India and its reliance upon the West during the years since it got its supposed independence, has it today just as helpless and dependent as it was when it first got its independence. Whereas in China, the Chinese fought for their independence. They became militant right from the outstart, and today they're—even though they aren't loved, they are, they are respected. Though the West doesn't love them, the West respects them. Now, the West doesn't respect India, but it loves India."

Malcolm also used China's international strength as an example to demonstrate his view that Africa's independence would help to increase the respect accorded to African Americans. Malcolm explained: "The Chinese used to be disrespected. They used to use that expression in this country: 'You don't have a Chinaman's chance.' You remember that? You don't hear it lately. Because a Chinaman's got more chance than they have now. Why? Because China is strong. Since China became strong and independent, she's respected, she's recognized. So wherever a Chinese person goes, he is respected and he is recognized."

China was not the only Asian nation which Malcolm made reference to. Malcolm explained of the Japanese: "The Japanese on some of those islands in the Pacific, when the American soldiers landed, one Japanese sometimes could hold the whole army off. He'd just wait until the sun went down, and when the sun went down they were all equal. He would take his little blade and slip from bush to bush, and from American to American. The white soldiers couldn't cope with that." In the same speech, Malcolm also referred to the defeat of the French in French Indochina. He explained: "People who just a few years previously were rice farmers got together and ran the heavily-mechanized French army out of Indochina."

Malcolm saw the struggles of African Americans as part of a larger international struggle against Western hegemony and aggression towards the non-white people of the world. He looked to the struggles which Asian people were engaged in as a source of inspiration. He was not the only African to look to China. The Black Panther Party, which adopted the ideology of Marxism-Leninism, looked to Mao as a source of ideological inspiration. Mao appealed to African people not only racially because he was a non-white revolutionary leader, but also ideologically because Mao's revolution was a Marxist inspired revolution which sought to overthrow the capitalist system which was exploiting people throughout the world.

The Black Panther Party looked to Frantz Fanon as well. In a document titled "On the Ideology of the

Black Panther Party," Eldridge Cleaver elaborated on the ideology of the Black Panther Party. He explained that the Black Panther Party viewed the struggle of black people in America through the prism of Marxism-Leninism. The Panther's embrace of Marxism-Leninism was inspired largely by Frantz Fanon. In Cleaver's view, Fanon was the first major Marxist-Leninist theoretician "who was primarily concerned about Black people, wherever they may be found." Cleaver added that Fanon was primarily focused on Africa and that it "is only indirectly that his works are beneficial to Afro-Americans." Cleaver also noted that "Fanon delivered a devastating attack upon Marxism-Leninism for its narrow preoccupation with Europe and the affairs and salvation of White folks, while lumping all third world peoples into the category of the Lumpenproletariat and then forgetting them there; Fanon unearthed the category of the Lumpenproletariat and began to deal with it, recognizing that vast majorities of the colonized people fall into that category." Mao, Fanon, and others helped to challenge the notion that Marxism was merely a "white thing."

What also helped to challenge the abovementioned notion was the class stratification which was produced in colonial societies due to the influence of colonialism and capitalism. As was noted before, the class which seized power was a class which was not only alienated from the masses culturally, but this was also a class which was fully willingly to align with international capitalist powers to exploit the masses.

In "Crisis in the Periphery: Africa and the Caribbean," Rodney addressed the issue of which class was to devise and implement the program for change. He explained that in African and Caribbean societies there were two components which had power. The first of which were the working people, whose power came from their production, although in most cases this was a potential power which was yet to be actualized. The other group with power was the group which controlled the state. This group controlled the allocation of resources and the allocation of surplus in the society. The latter group Rodney referred to as the petty (or petit) bourgeoisie—this was the class to which Rodney himself belonged to. Thomas Sankara, the former president of Burkina Faso, had described the petty bourgeoisie as a class which "often vacillates between the cause of the popular masses and that of imperialism. In its large majority, it always ends up by taking the side of the popular masses."

In Rodney's view, the working class should be the leading social group in the struggle. In his view, the petty bourgeoisie as a class is unable to lead a country anywhere except to destruction since that class was spawned from imperialism and capitalism within colonial societies.

Rodney also rejected the socialist ideologies which were espoused by leaders who belonged to the petty bourgeoisie class. Rodney's position was that the socialist ideologies of Kwame Nkrumah, Sékou Touré, Julius Nyerere, and Michael Manley did not go far enough in transforming social relations in post-colonial societies because these leaders had already established the hegemony of the petty bourgeoisie over the working class.

Nkrumah belonged to what Rodney referred to as the "vanguard" of the Pan-African movement which emerged from the Fifth Pan-African Congress. Rodney stated that this vanguard lost its direction and wallowing "in bourgeois theory and practice." Rodney cited the example of George Padmore, "who propagated the false antithesis between Pan-Africanism and Communism" and as a result of this Padmore's "practical politics suffered a corresponding decline" to the point that Padmore found himself intervening in Guyana on behalf of the local leadership that was supported by the British and American governments, as well as a CIA infiltrated trade union known as the American Federation of Labor and Congress of Industrial Organizations (AFL-CIO).

Rodney certainly was not the only Marxist to raise these critiques of Padmore. Paul Trewhela wrote an article for *Searchlight South Africa* which was titled "George Padmore: A Critique. Pan-Africanism or Marxism?" Padmore was born Malcolm Nurse in Trinidad. He joined the Communist Party in the 1920s while he was living in the United States, but he eventually broke with the Communist Party over its policy towards the colonial powers. Padmore then shifted his energy towards Pan-Africanism. He was one of the organizers of the Fifth Pan-African Conference in 1945. Of Padmore's break with the Comintern, C.L.R. James wrote: "In 1935, seeking alliances, the Kremlin separated Britain and France as 'democratic imperialisms' from Germany and Japan, making the 'Fascist imperialisms' the main target of Russian and Communist propaganda. This reduced activity for African emancipation to a farce: Germany and Japan had no colonies in Africa. Padmore broke instantly with the Kremlin."

Trewhela noted that Padmore broke with the Soviet Union at a time when "the Marxist programme was openly abandoned by the Soviet leadership, in its vain hope of appeasing British, French and US imperialism in face of the danger from nazi Germany." Trewhela's criticism of Padmore is that whereas Leon Trotsky reacted to the developments in the Soviet Union by demanding for the renewal of Marxist internationalism, Padmore shifted his focus to the emancipation of colonized peoples.

The problem with Padmore's shift in focus was that he came to believe that independence for the colonized nations could be achieved through working with the colonial powers. He put forward this argument in *White Man's Duty* in which Padmore argued that "Britain, by freeing her Colonies, can save both herself and them and lay the foundations of a new Commonwealth of Nations, bound together in equal partnership". In *The Gold Coast Revolution*, Padmore called for the British parliament to "restore faith" among Africans by giving its colonies Dominion status within the Commonwealth. These remarks demonstrated that Padmore himself still held faith in British colonialism.

It is clear that Padmore's brand of Pan-Africanism was not a revolutionary anti-imperialist brand, but one which sought to achieve Africa's independence through a mutual relationship with the very colonial powers which had oppressed African people. It would appear that Padmore had used anti-communism as a means to secure some form of leverage with British imperialism by urging British imperialism to act to prevent Africans from turning to communism. In doing so, Padmore was expressing the view that

Africa's future was in the control of Western nations and that it would be the actions of Western nations which would dictate Africa's attitudes.

Rodney accused Kwame Nkrumah of "engaging in ideological mystification" with his new ideology of consciencism, "while doing little to break the control of the international bourgeoisie or the Ghanaian petty bourgeoisie over the state."

Rodney was particularly critical of Nkrumah's missteps in Ghana. Rodney pointed out that Nkrumah's ideology was constantly shifting and that Nkrumah was "searching for an ideology." Rodney explained that Nkrumah started with a mixture of Marxism and Protestantism, and then moved to Consciencism and then Nkrumahism. In Rodney's view, Nkrumah's shifting ideologies were rooted in Nkrumah's desire to "avoid the trap of adopting something alien." In doing so, Rodney argued that Nkrumah had also refused to accept the class contradictions that existed in Ghana and continued to do so until he was overthrown by the petty bourgeoisie class. For this reason, Rodney concluded that Nkrumah's text *Class Struggle in Africa* was significant because this text was "the closest that Nkrumah comes to a self-critique." For Rodney, Nkrumah's hesitancy to outright embrace scientific socialism was one of the factors that led to his being overthrown in Ghana.

Walter Rodney pointed out that in post-colonial Africa, many leaders rejected democracy. Rodney explained that these leaders had taken a specific type of "bourgeois democracy" and presented it as the absolute form of democracy, thereby rejecting the entire concept. Instead, these states adopted a "species of authoritarianism" in which working people were effectively unable to make choices within the society.

Some African leaders argued that having a single-state party was necessary because having too many parties could create division. President Joseph Momoh of Sierra Leone explained: "As your president, I have to say it loud and clear—multi-partyism at this point of our social and economic development will only spell doom for us and take us right back to those old dangerous days of divisiveness, conflict, victimisation and vindictiveness that we have happily left behind for well over a decade." He also added that "the principle and practice of the system of popular participation under the one-party democracy over the years has proved to be very useful." In Cameroon, Paul Biya denounced the demands for multiple parties as a diversion from the country's economic crisis. He also applauded party loyalists for organizing pro-government demonstrations.

In some cases, regimes which established one-party rule even called themselves democratic. Sékou Touré's party in Guinea was known as the Democratic Party of Guinea. The suppression of certain rights and the abuses which took place under Touré's rule was justified as being necessary to protect the revolution in Guinea from imperialist forces. There is no denying that there were imperialist forces who were seeking to overthrow the government of Guinea, as had been done to Nkrumah in Ghana. The problem was that in the end, despite the use of brutal force against Guinean citizens, the regime in Guinea ultimately ended up adopting a position which was pro-Western and pro-capitalist.

Touré, an avowed socialist, eventually reconciled with the Western capitalistic nations in his later years. In 1982, Touré visited New York to encourage Western businessmen to invest in Guinea. Touré had denounced Felix Houphouët-Boigny of the Ivory Coast as being a neo-colonialist, but the year before Touré's death Houphouët-Boigny described Touré as a close friend and he touted Guinea as an example of the pro-Western approach towards economic and political development in Africa. When Touré died in 1984 he received various tributes from Western leaders and their African allies who defended their relationship with Touré. The *New York Times* reported: "He had been mellowing, Western diplomats and African conservatives said. He was no longer resorting to violent oppression as easily or often as he had in the past, they asserted."

Tanzania under Nyerere was also subjected to similar forms of repression. John S. Saul offered multiple accounts of these types of abuses. He recounted the case of Simon Akivaga, the leader of the University Student Council at the University of Dar es Salaam, who was dragged away at gunpoint and then expelled from the nation. His crime was apparently criticizing the university's structure. Other faculty members who sided with the students were also disciplined. Arnold Temu of the History Department was thrown out of Parliament and then removed from the university when he questioned the regime's handling of university issues. Saul stated: "Thus, for all his own suspicion of the Soviet Union, Nyerere embraced, for Tanzania itself, much the same vanguard party model as the Soviets exemplified—even if he sought to sweeten that system with an ingenious (too ingenious?) innovation of his own: 'one-party democracy.'"

Rodney confronted this very issue in Guyana under the government of Burnham. In 1974, Burnham declared the paramountcy of the People's National Congress (PNC) over the government. This meant that leadership at all levels of the country should be in the hands of the PNC, which became "the major national institution." Burnham held the view that the "government has got to be in our system a subordinate agency of the party." The government was further subordinated by Burnham's decision to rig elections and utilize violence against political opponents.

As Rodney pointed out, the "choice of production" in post-colonial societies was determined not within those societies themselves, but by the "metropolitan core economies." The pattern of production in post-colonial societies remained exporting products which those societies themselves do not consume. This is what was done in Guinea at the expense of the working people. The socialism which many post-colonial leaders preached did not bring about a significant transformation in this system of production.

I quote Sankara again, who explained that "the educated petty bourgeoisie of Africa—if not the Third World—is not prepared to give up its privileges, either due to intellectual laziness or simply because it has tasted the Western way of life." For this reason, the petty bourgeoisie often became an obstacle in the way of genuine liberation.

The end of colonialism in Africa and the Caribbean did not bring about the type of fundamental transformations which were needed. Many of the post-colonial leaders retained the same basic features of the colonial society, which was a society in which the working class remained poor and exploited, while laboring for the benefit of wealthy capitalist nations. The significance of Walter Rodney's assessment of post-colonial society is that he understood this transformation could only come from the workers and the peasants, who made up the masses of the post-colonial society, and who were also the most neglected and exploited segment of post-colonial society.

2 NATIONALISM VERSUS MARXISM

One of the major ideological debates in the struggle for African freedom that emerged in the 1920s and remained a hotly debated issue within the global African struggle until the end of the Cold War was the question of race and class; whether Black Nationalism or Marxism would lead to black liberation. The issue would not be as hotly debated given the general decline of the prominence of Marxism/socialism in public discourse after the fall of the Soviet Union, but the issue has not gone away altogether.

First it is essential to define the two ideologies. Martin Delany is often called the Father of Black Nationalism because he articulated many of the views which would become identified with Black Nationalism. Delany described black people as a "nation within a nation" similar to the "Poles in Russia, the Hungarians in Austria, the Welsh, Irish, and Scotch in the British dominions." For Delany it was especially important for black people to see themselves as a collective nation because the "claims of no people, according to established policy and usage, are respected by any nation, until they are presented in a national capacity."

Generally speaking, Black Nationalism tends to view black people as a distinction nation and advocates for either the creation of a separate black nation in the United States or for the complete control of black communities. Malcolm X gave the following definition of Black Nationalism: "My personal economic philosophy is also Black Nationalism, which means that the black man should have a hand in controlling the economy of the so-called Negro community, he should be developing the type of knowledge that will enable him to own and operate the businesses and thereby be able to create employment for his own people, for his own kind. And the social philosophy also is Black Nationalism, which means that instead of the black man trying to force himself into the society of the white man, we should be trying to eliminate from our own society the ills and the defects and make ourselves likable and sociable among our own kind."

Malcolm was defining Black Nationalism as a belief that black people should have economic control of their community in order to solve their own social problems, rather than depending on white people to solve their problems for them. As I noted, others have defined nationalism in terms of creating a separate state. This was the position of the Nation of Islam and the Republic of New Afrika.

On the other side of the debate is Marxism. Whereas Black Nationalism is concerned with the economic self-reliance and empowerment of black people, Marxism is strictly a class assessment. The theories of Karl Marx and Friedrich Engels gave birth to what is termed Marxism or communism. This position essentially argues that capitalism is a stage of history in which the ruling class (the bourgeoisie) enriches itself through exploiting the labor of the working class (the proletariat). Marxism argues that history transitions from one stage to the next and that in time the working class will rise up and overthrow the ruling class, thus transitioning away from capitalism and creating a communist society. This is a stateless and classless society in which there is a common ownership of the means of production, so that workers directly reap the benefits of their labor rather than working for wages from their bosses. There are also offshoots of Marxism such as Marxism-Leninism, Trotskyism, Maoism, and Marxism-Leninism-Maoism.

The most immediate issue that Marxism has in relation to the African struggle is that as an ideology it concerns itself with the historical development of Europe. In *How Europe Underdeveloped Africa*, Walter Rodney explained that Marx's historical stages of development could not be applied to Africa given that Europe and Africa followed different trajectories of historical development—for example, African societies tended to be more communal than European societies, which were often very harsh in enforcing the concept of private ownership. Marx also did not address the issue of racism or European imperialism in Africa in any significant way, so Marxism poses an issue in the African struggle because it was not created with Africans in mind. It was an ideology (some would say science) that emerged in Europe to assess the historical development of the class structure in Europe. Rodney recognized this limitation and argued that Marxism could not be applied wholesale to the African struggle.

Nationalists have tended to dismiss Marxism partly because of its seeming irrelevance to the African struggle due to the fact that Marxism emerged out of European society as an analysis of the class structure in Europe. This was precisely the critique which Molefi Asante raised. Asante claimed that "Marxism acts on the same Eurocentric base as capitalism because for both life is economics, not culture. The class-warrior attitude dominates the thinking of Marxists and capitalists. It is a war of class against class, group against group, and individual against individual.... This, of course, is contradictory to the Afrocentric value which respects difference and applauds pluralism. Strangers exist in that they have not been known."

Nationalists have also dismissed Marxism due not only to the racism of white people, but also out of a skepticism appeals to class unity could overcome such racism. In his book *The Psychopathic Racial Personality and Other Essays*, Bobby E. Wright argued that one of the dilemmas that Africans faced was that their "appeal for liberation" was through channels that were created by white people, "namely democracy and communism (Marxism)." Wright further wrote: "For communism to be viable requires the cooperation of the masses of the White race. With that as the primary condition, communism needs no further consideration."

Robert F. Williams, who was himself a nationalist, expressed similar reservations about communism when he was in exile in Cuba. Williams found that the Cubans were opposed to nationalism. Williams explained, "they had a black population in Cuba and they did not want these ideas to catch on among their people." Alberto Benvenuti explained: "Despite the fact that Williams maintained good relations with Castro and Guevara, many Cuban communists ostracized his work. The communists—who were gaining influence within the Cuban government as a consequence of the alliance between Cuba and the Soviet Union—feared that Williams, who was a non-communist black revolutionary, would inspire separatist sentiments among Afro-Cubans, in particular in the Oriente province, which had a numerous black population."

Williams explained that the view of the leaders in Cuba was that "the race issue in America is due to class oppression, that this class struggle, rather than racial struggle, and the Cubans maintained that—in fact, they insisted that the white workers are being exploited in the United States and the white workers, the working class, is a natural ally of the black people and that eventually the white workers will—the working class will unite with the black people and that they will bring about the necessary changes to improve conditions for all people including the black people." Williams was not convinced, however. Williams expressed the view that as long as white workers "have jobs and can buy automobiles and homes, they've no real reason to rise up against the capitalists. Only those like, like us Blacks, who are victims of severe economic discrimination and racism, have the motivation to want to overthrow the system." Williams also could not help but notice the racism in Cuba. When he went to Radio Havana, he noticed that all of the faces there were white. He found the same thing in the foreign ministry. Williams noted that some black Cubans were eventually brought into the foreign ministry, but the people they got were not qualified.

The issues which Williams observed in Cuba is relevant to the case of Walterio Carbonell, who was a revolutionary writer and intellectual who supported the Cuban revolution. Carbonell ran into issues with the Cuban government over his position that the contributions of Afro-Cubans should be acknowledged. In 1961, he published a book entitled *How Our National Culture Emerged*, which was a book that examined the role that enslaved Africans played in the creation of Cuba's culture. Carbonell called for a reevaluation of the "creators of Cuban nationality," who were all white.

One of the arguments which Carbonell put forward was that the national music of Cuba was African. He wrote: "Way before the Revolution, the bourgeoisie was already quite compromised by imperialism, not only in terms of economic power but also in terms of cultural power, too. In addition, its cultural values had been undermined by black traditions and practices. This is how African musical rhythms, considered savage by the bourgeoisie until 1930, the very same musical rhythm of the colonial slave quarters, rhythms that garnered slaves a hundred lashes from their owners, in punishment, became the bourgeoisie's preferred and most entertaining dance beat." Carbonell went so far as to argue that the music of the white population in Cuba disappeared and was replaced by black music.

Carbonell also wrote about the cultural clash between Africans and Europeans in Cuba, explaining:

"The evidence that the conflicts of the Spanish colonial era were not just economic and political is that after the end of Spanish domination the musical and religious habits and customs of the white and black populations continued to be at odds. During the republican period the struggle between the black African and white Spanish cultures continues. The dialectical conflict between Spanish culture and African culture in Cuba has ended in a victory for black music over the music of the old colonizers, even a victory of the collective psychology of blacks over the social psychology of the Spanish."

Of African religion in Cuba, Carbonell wrote: "Another symptom of weakness in the bourgeois culture is the way in which it allowed itself to become contaminated by black religious beliefs. The savage deities who ate children, Changó, Obatalá, Yemayá, got civilized and took over the spirits of wealthy people not to devour them nor live with them but to try to solve their romantic problems, help them in their aspiration to occupy high governmental positions, or get them out of difficult business situations." He further explained: "The bourgeoisie did not find enough magic in its own religion to solve its economic problems: the more the country's economic instability grew, the more African beliefs took hold in the minds of the dominant class." Carbonell also held the view that "religious organizations played a progressive role in the political and cultural aspects of our nationality" and that the notions of African religions being savagery was "espoused by colonial ideologues and their followers, the reactionary bourgeoisie."

In Carbonell's view, wherever African and

European cultures in Cuba clashed, it was African culture which prevailed. This demonstrated to Carbonell the strength of African culture, but also the weakness of white bourgeois culture in Cuba. Carbonell also argued that because "the slaves, the most exploited class, who fueled the colonial economy and were the longest suffering during the nineteenth century (from 1800 till the Zanjón Treaty), it was from them that the more revolutionary classes emerged. This Marxist conclusion is confirmed by the very revolutionary actions of the Cuban slaves."

Carbonell explained to a Cuban journalist that at the time he wrote his book his ideas were plagued by a sense of urgency because Cuba was in the early years of the revolution and he wanted to contribute to the success of the revolutionary ideas. Here, Carbonell might have gone too far even for some of the revolutionaries in Cuba. José Hugo Fernández explained that "Carbonell's reservations about the so-called 'founders of the Cuban nationality' promised to be more defiant and revolutionary than the revolution itself (at least that is how they were received by most, if not all)." Carbonell himself recognized that certain bourgeois notions about culture in Cuba were held by some of the revolutionaries. He explained that "the bourgeoisie established its authority not only on economic and political power, but also on the power of the lies their cultured men issued forth. In addition, because today many of those lies are held as true, even by the revolutionaries, and have contributed to liberating our country from bourgeois domination, but have been incapable of liberating themselves from the power of bourgeois ideology."

Carbonell's views isolated him in Cuba. He was

labeled as being mentally deficient and relegated to working in a corner at the José Martí National Library. Fernández explained that Carbonell "died in Havana in isolation, mercilessly squashed, desperately poor, but still supporting the revolution, which he loved unconditionally and uncritically, even though hopeless." This is significant to me because Carbonell was a Marxist-Leninist who supported the revolution in Cuba. He was not someone who sought to overturn the revolution. He remained committed to Marxism-Leninism and the revolution in Cuba to the very end, but there was no place in the revolution for him because of the ideas which he proposed.

The revolution in Cuba made some important strides in addressing the issue of racial discrimination. Afro-Cubans such as Juan Almeida Bosque have played a significant role in this process as well. Assata Shakur, who fled to Cuba to escape political repression in the United States, noted that many Cubans told her that racism did not exist in Cuba and that racism was illegal in Cuba. The reality was, however, that after decades of being in power in Cuba, Castro had failed to eliminate racism from Cuba. A large reason for this failure is that Castro himself seemed to have underestimated to have underestimated how deeply entrenched racism in Cuban society was. Communism addresses issues of class relations and class exploitation, but racism in Cuba was more complex than being a mere class issue.

Rodney expressed similar views as well. He stated that it "has long been recognized that the white working class in the U.S.A is historically incapable of participating (as a class) in anti-imperialist struggle."

He continued to explain that organized labor in the United States had become a "reactionary force."

Indeed, there has been a lengthy history of racism coming from organized labor in the United States. This was why in 1959 the black members of the American Federation of Labor and Congress of Industrial Organizations (AFL–CIO) had to form their own Negro American Labor Council (NALC) under the leadership of A. Philip Randolph. Randolph complained: "It is unfortunate that some of our liberal friends, along with some of the leaders of labor, even yet do not comprehend the nature, scope, depth, and challenge of this civil rights revolution which is surging forward in the House of Labor." The reality is that when you look at American history, you will find numerous examples of the white working class struggling for their own advancement with little regard to the struggles of African people.

Samuel Gompers, who served as the president of the AFL, wrote a pamphlet in 1901 in which he argued against "the admission of Asiatics" to the United States. On a separate occasion, he warned about "the menace of a possible overwhelming of our people by hordes of Asiatics." The A.F.L. was meant to be an organization which sought to unite working people regardless of their color or nationality, but Gompers barred the admission of Chinese and Japanese members. Gompers defended his position by claiming that he had no prejudice against Chinese people. He claimed to have a "profound respect for the Chinese nation." He opposed Chinese immigration because of the "ills they would bring to the country." Gompers is an example of the fact that for many labor organizers in the United States, race was a more important social category than class.

As was stated the fundamental difference between the nationalists and the Marxists came down to the question over the relevancy of Marx's theories to African people given the historical differences and the racism of the white working class. It could be argued that there was validity in both positions. This can be demonstrated by the ideological clash that the Black Panther Party had with "cultural nationalists" in the 1960s.

In an interview, Huey Newton used Francois Duvalier of Haiti as an example of the problems with cultural nationalists: "The cultural nationalists are concerned with returning to the old African culture and thereby regaining their identity and freedom. In other words, they feel that African culture will automatically bring political freedom. Many times cultural nationalists fall into line as reactionary nationalists. 'Papa Doc' in Haiti is an excellent example of reactionary nationalism. He oppresses the people but he does promote the African culture. He is against anything other than black, which on the surface seems very good, but to him it is only to mislead the people. He merely kicked out the racists and replaced them with himself as the oppressor. Many of the nationalists in this country seem to desire the same ends."

The Panthers rightfully recognized that the rhetoric of the cultural nationalists was one which promoted African identity and culture, but that cultural nationalists often took political positions which supported the very system which kept African people oppressed. This is why H. Rap Brown explained: "When you begin to stress culture without politics, people can become so hooked up in the beauty of themselves that they have no desire to fight. It becomes ego-gratifying just to be Black. Vanguard groups can't afford to go around stressing culture without politics, the real test now is preparation for, and initiation of, struggle. Write me a novel about how to infiltrate the FBI and destroy it. Write me poems that say more than that you are Black and beautiful. Perform dances with guns to legitimatize guns as a weapon of struggle."

Just as it has been demonstrated that those preaching a message of cultural nationalism are not necessarily coming from a revolutionary and progressive approach, one should not make the mistake of totally neglecting the aspect of African culture in the struggle for African liberation. Given that the stripping of African culture was a critical aspect of the oppression of African people, the struggle against oppression is in part a cultural one. This seemed to have been one of the greatest weaknesses of the Panthers. Assata Shakur pointed out that the political education program of the Panthers often left their followers with a limited understanding of their own history: "They were reading the *Red Book* but didn't know who Harriet Tubman, Marcus Garvey, and Nat Turner were. They talked about intercommunalism but still really believed that the Civil War was fought to free the slaves. A whole lot of them barely understood any kind of history, Black, African, or otherwise."

Not only did members lack a serious historical understanding of the African struggle in the United States, but they also had a skewed understanding of political struggle. Many believed that the struggle only consisted of "picking up the gun and serving the people." Shakur explained that many people "joined thinking the Party was going to issue them a gun and direct them to go out and shoot pigs." Noting that many of the people who joined the Panthers attended poor schools that taught them very little, if anything at all, Shakur felt that the Panthers should have done more to educate its members. America was not Russia and it was not China, so studying Lenin and studying Mao, but neglecting to study Tubman or Garvey is to be completely unprepared to truly address the struggles of African people in the United States.

Whereas the "cultural nationalists" concerned themselves with African history and African culture, the Black Panther Party was more preoccupied with developing a revolutionary political theory. The problem was that the Panthers did not adopt an approach which was centered on the historical, social, and cultural experiences of African people. Some within the Black Panther Party, such as Shakur, did embrace African culture. This is demonstrated by the fact that Shakur took on an African name. The general focus of the Black Panther Party, however, was not developing a sense of African pride or identity among its membership.

During the revolutionary struggle in the 1960s many of the leaders of the period were struggling to develop a clear and effective ideological approach. This struggle was at the root of the differences between the Black Panther Party and those who embraced cultural nationalism. The Black Panthers adopted a more politically revolutionary approach than most cultural nationalists, but this was an approach which was somewhat disconnected from the historical and cultural experiences of African Americans.

Though the two positions seem contrary, the reality is that it is possible to reconcile a position which views the struggle of African people both in terms of class and in terms of race. This is demonstrated by Marcus Garvey, who was also a nationalist.

Garvey's speeches and writings are filled with references to class struggles and even at times appeals to working class solidarity. In 1924, Garvey complained: "We have not only to fight the white capitalist, but we also have to fight the capitalistic Negro. He will sell his own people into Hell the same as anybody else." Garvey was very critical of those wealthy black men who were "money hoarders" that did little to help their race. In a 1926 editorial, Garvey wrote: "The royal and privileged classes of idlers who used to tyrannize and oppress the humble hordes of mankind are now experiencing difficulty in holding their control over the sentiment of the people." Though Garvey was a self-professed supporter of capitalism, he also recognized that the capitalist class was a class which exploited the masses for profit.

Thomas Sankara stands out among the African leaders who embraced the Marxist ideology for two reasons. The first of which was that he was not dogmatic in his approach to Marxism. In fact, Sankara did not consider himself to be a Marxist, although he had read both Marx and Lenin, and was clearly influenced by the thinking of both men. Whereas the revolutionary government of Grenada was supportive of the Soviet Union to the point of supporting the Soviet invasion of Afghanistan, Sankara expressed his support of the Afghan people as they fought against the Soviets. Secondly, Sankara supported economic self-reliance in an attempt to break Burkina Faso's dependency on Western foreign aid and Western goods. Although he did not call himself a Black Nationalist, economic self-reliance is an aspect of Black Nationalist thinking. Sankara's views were very similar to that of Martin Delany and Marcus Garvey, so much so that all three shared the sentiment of Africa for African people—the precise wording of that phrase differed between the three men, but all three of them uttered a different variation of the same phrase. Sankara was also a committed Pan-Africanist who worked to build bridges with African Americans and to unite Africa. He saw himself as someone who was carrying on the legacy of Nkrumah's Pan-African vision.

In conclusion, I would argue that Marxism and Black Nationalism do not necessarily have to be rivaling or competing ideologies, as we have seen leaders adopt aspects of both. With that being established, I would also argue that Black Nationalism has produced more results among African people for the various reasons that were listed above. Where we do find Africans who were effective in adopting Marxist thought, they are usually those like Walter Rodney or Thomas Sankara who were also Pan-Africanists who espoused positions that would fall under Malcolm X's description of Black Nationalism.

3 MARXISM IN THE AFRICAN CONTEXT

After relocating to Guinea, Stokely Carmichael adopted the name Kwame Ture and became a member of the All-African People's Revolutionary Party. As an activist in the United States, Ture called for Black Power. The concept of Black Power was articulated in a book which Ture co-wrote with Charles Hamilton. After moving to Guinea, Ture adopted the ideology of Nkrumahism-Toureism which was based on the political ideologies of Kwame Nkrumah of Ghana and Sekou Toure of Guinea. One of the most important aspects of Nkrumahism-Toureism as espoused by Kwame Ture is the importance of placing the culture of African people at the center of the Pan-African liberation struggle. Nkrumahism-Toureism is a socialist ideology rooted in the historical and cultural experiences of African people. In this regard, Nkrumahism-Toureism distinguishes itself from other anti-capitalist ideologies such as Marxism, Marxism-Leninism, and Maoism.

Ture saw the tendency towards unification as being an innate evolutionary process which was interrupted by colonialism and slavery. As such, Ture argued that the unification of Africa could now only be obtained through a revolutionary process rather than an evolutionary one. Indeed, throughout Africa there was a process of nation building which produced large multiethnic kingdoms. In West Africa, several large multi-ethnic empires had emerged, such as the empires of Mali and Songhai. In South Africa, Dingizwayo was working towards uniting the disunited and warring tribes. Dingizwayo served as a mentor for Shaka who would later develop the Zulu Empire. These are just some examples to illustrate the point which Ture made. Walter Rodney explained: "All of the large states of nineteenth-century Africa were multiethnic, and their expansion was continually making anything like 'tribal' loyalty a thing of the past, by substituting in its place national and class ties."

Not only did colonialism disrupt Africa's development, but it also forced the creation of new nations in Africa. These new nations conformed to the borders which were established during colonialism. One area of conflict that Kwame Ture had with Marxist-Leninists was on the question of nationalism. Marxist-Leninists denounced nationalism, but in Ture's view nationalism was positive in situations where people went from being a state to a nation.

Former African colonies had to become nations as part of their struggle for liberation. This was noted by Julius Nyerere who complained that he was often seen as being an African rather than a Tanzanian. He illustrated this in a speech in which he mentioned that people asked him about the problems in Rwanda. Nyerere pointed out that it would have never occurred to him to ask Tony Blair about the war in Bosnia or to ask Helmut Kohl about the war in Chechnya, but Nyerere was asked about Rwanda because Westerners failed to distinguish between Rwanda and Tanzania. Nyerere continued to explain that the Europeans and North Americans were correct for viewing him as an African because Tanzania was a nation which he created. Tanzania was formed as a union between Tanganyika and Zanzibar following the revolution in Zanzibar. Nyerere wanted East Africa to be unified at independence rather than becoming independent as separate states. Nyerere even argued that Tanganyika should delay its independence to unite with other East African states at independence. This did not happen, which merely made the process of establishing political unity in East Africa more challenging.

Another area where Ture and Marxist-Leninists had differences was on the question of religion. Ture recognized that not only are African people deeply religious, but Africans often used religion as a tool in their struggle for liberation. He mentioned Martin Luther King and Malcolm X as two examples. For this reason, he did not preach atheism as being a necessary aspect of the revolutionary struggle as certain Marxist-Leninists did. Ture noted the irony of the fact that the Communist Party USA advocated that atheism was a fundamental aspect of the struggle for freedom, but the only place in the south the Communist Party USA could organize was in the church. Ture himself organized in the church when he was working with the Student Non-Violent Coordinating Committee.

Kwame Ture was not the only Pan-Africanist socialist who looked outside of Marxism for his ideology. Julius Nyerere of Tanzania did the same thing. Nyerere viewed African societies as being fundamentally socialistic. This is evident when he writes: "We, in Africa, have no more need of being 'converted' to socialism than we have of being 'taught' democracy. Both are rooted in our own past—in the traditional society which produced us." In locating socialism within traditional African culture, Nyerere also sought to distance his socialism from other forms of socialism. Nyerere's brand of socialism was also not rooted in the historic class struggle that Karl Marx theorized. In fact, Nyerere criticized European socialism for viewing civil war (referring to class war) as a good thing. He writes: "As prayer is to Christianity or to Islam, so civil war (which they call 'class war') is to the European version of socialism—a means inseparable from the end. Each becomes the basis of a whole way of life. The European socialist cannot think of his socialism without its father—Capitalism!"

This was a contradiction that Nyerere considered to be intolerable. For him European socialism practically stated: "Without capitalism, and the conflict which capitalism creates within society, there can be no socialism!" Nyerere doubted whether or not any African language even had a word for class. Nyerere further argued: "The foundation, and the objective, of African socialism is the extended family. The true African socialist does not look on one class of men as his brethren and another as his natural enemies. He does not form an alliance with the 'brethren' for the extermination of the 'non-brethren'."

Walter Rodney had addressed some of the challenges with adopting Marxism to cultures outside of Europe. One of the aspects of Rodney's analysis of Marxism was that it was pragmatic, rather than dogmatic. Robert Hill explained: "At the forefront of his analysis was always the concern to eschew labels and dogma of any kind and his search for a resolution of problems in actual practice." This was partly due to the fact that Rodney recognized that Marxism was not an ideology that one could apply uncritically towards any situation since Marxism was a social science that emerged out of the context of European society. He certainly recognized that the historical stages of the development in Europe were not the same as those in Africa: "Both Marxists and non-Marxists alike (with different motivations) have pointed out that the sequences of modes of production noted in Europe were not reproduced in Africa. In Africa, after the communal stage there was no epoch of slavery arising out of internal evolution. Nor was there a mode of production that was the replica of European feudalism. Marx himself recognized that the stages of development in Asia had produced a form of society which could not easily be fitted into a European slot."

Rodney had earlier noted the differences in economic development between Europe and Africa. In *The Groundings with my Brothers*, Rodney wrote: "Even within the empires of Ghana, Mali and Songhai, the explosiveness of class contradictions was lacking, as Diop stresses in his *Nations Negres et Culture*. In the states of Ashante and Dahomey, whose growth was contemporaneous with European mercantilism, there was no concept of the 'market' in the sense of supply and demand, and the social redistribution of goods made accumulation impossible."

Rodney argued that Marxism was a tool of analysis that had to be applied differently based on the situation: "Marxism is not just a study of some classic texts written for some other situation. We should enter into the spirit of the analysis and be capable of applying it creatively to our own situation." Rodney's views on Marxism were influenced by Amilcar Cabral, who waged a war for independence against the Portuguese in Guinea-Bissau. Cabral's formulation of Marxism included an assessment of Guinea-Bissau's own history, using Marx's method. Cabral pointed out that class formulation occurred later in Guinea-Bissau's history than it did in Europe, which was the society that Marx was primarily concerned with. The significance of Cabral's application of Marxian methodology for Rodney was that Cabral demonstrated "the relevance of that methodology to African society."

Rodney also argued that what Cabral did in Guinea-Bissau was essentially what Vladimir Lenin did in Russia or what Mao Tse-tung did in China. Both men took the doctrine of Marxism and applied it to the specific situation in their countries. Rodney explained that Lenin "had to take those formulations out of the specific cultural and historical context of Western Europe and look at Eastern Europe, at Russia which was evolving differently, and apply them to his own society." He points out that Mao did the same in China, where Mao was "applying it to Chinese society which was a different society from Russian society."

Rodney's analysis on African American political prisoner George Jackson is a testament to his interest in the global struggles of African people and his pragmatic application of Marxist analysis. Jackson was jailed for stealing seventy dollars and during his time in prison he educated himself, just as Malcolm X had done. Jackson's newfound insight into the American political system brought him into conflict with the prison guards. Jackson being a political prisoner in jail was also significant to Rodney because "a significant proportion of African nationalist leaders graduated from colonialist prisons, and right now the jails of South Africa hold captive some of the best of our brothers in that part of the continent." Rodney explained that jail "is hardly an arena in which one would imagine that guerrilla warfare would take place." Despite this, Rodney noted that jail was precisely the arena in which Jackson waged his struggle against the oppressive system.

Rodney also understood that the significance of someone like Jackson was that it proved that the African lumpen proletariat was a potential revolutionary force, despite the fact that Karl Marx had described such a group as having been so cut off from the system of production that they did not understand the functions of the society that oppressed them. For this reason, the lumpen was unlikely to ever obtain the proper class consciousness needed to become part of the revolutionary struggle of the working class. Marx defined this class as including criminals, beggars, prostitutes, and others that engaged in criminal or degrading activities to make a living. Jackson, a criminal who self-identified as a member of the lumpen, proved that the African lumpen class in the United States was not to be dismissed as an element of the struggle in the same way that Marx had dismissed the lumpen in Europe.

Rodney was also critical of the role of white people

in the struggle of African people. Whereas many Marxists tended to see the struggle as purely a class struggle in which the white and black working class had a common struggle, Rodney identified differences between the two which made cooperation between the two groups challenging. In America, Rodney argued that it "has long been recognized that the white working class in the U.S.A is historically incapable of participating (as a class) in anti-imperialist struggle." He continued to explain that organized labor in the United States had become a "reactionary force."

Rodney recognized that in the debate over the relevance of Marxism to the African struggle one had to address the question of Marxism being a foreign ideology. Rodney pointed out: "In many respects, when we ask the question today about the relevance of Marxism to black people, we have already reached a minority position, as it were. Many of those engaged in the debate present the debate as though Marxism is a European phenomenon and black people responding to it must of necessity be alienated because the alienation of race must enter into the discussion." Rodney argued that there is no distinction to be made from natural sciences and social sciences. For this reason, Rodney explained that people "have no difficulty in deciding that they are going to use facets of the material culture that originated in the West, whether it originated in capitalist or socialist society." For this reason, Africans would utilize electricity without questioning whether or not Thomas Edison was a racist, yet those same people would reject Marxism on the grounds of Marx being a racist. In this regard, Rodney was arguing that Marxism was a social science that emerged out of Europe, but still could be of use to African people in the same manner that European scientific creations were used by African people.

Of those Pan-African thinkers who were critical of Marxism, the psychologist Bobby E. Wright stands out. He argued that one of the dilemmas that Africans faced was that their "appeal for liberation" was through channels that were created by white people, "namely democracy and communism (Marxism)." Wright further wrote: "For communism to be viable requires the cooperation of the masses of the White race. With that as the primary condition, communism needs no further consideration." Wright dismissed Marxism simply on the grounds that it seemingly required cooperation with European people, but, as shall be demonstrated, Rodney's approach to Marxism could not be so simply dismissed on these grounds because his conception of Marxism was one that could exist independently from the white working class.

In Rodney's thinking there was no break between Marxism and Pan-Africanism because for Rodney the two ideologies complemented each other. This was especially important given the neo-colonial context which Rodney operated in. As was pointed out in the previous chapters, Rodney recognized that in the Caribbean and in Africa there was no genuine independence for the masses of black people. Instead, power was transferred, nominally, to a small class of politicians. The term nominally is used because, as Rodney so aptly explained, in post-colonial societies power still rested with the former colonizers.

4 RACE AND LABOR IN THE UNITED STATES SUPREME COURT

In *Psychopathic Racial Personality and Other Essays*, Bobby E. Wright argued that African Americans "are the world's only legally created group, (created through the 13th, 14th, and 15th amendments which can be repealed at any moment by the Congress or declared unconstitutional by the Supreme Court)." Wright's statement spoke to the very precarious legal situation which African Americans have been in. Congress has never repealed these amendments, but historically Congress has not consistently enforced the protections offered by these amendments. The Supreme Court has never declared the amendments unconstitutional, but the Supreme Court has certainly limited the protections offered by these amendments and has also limited the protections offered by civil rights legislation. In other words, Congress and the Supreme Court have not eliminated the legislation which was implemented to provide African Americans with the rights of citizenship, but such rights have been abridged so as to also protect the right of white people to discriminate as they see fit.

The Fourteenth Amendment was the amendment which provided citizenship for African Americans. The amendment reads:

> All persons born or naturalized in the United States, and subject to the jurisdiction thereof, are citizens of the United States and of the State wherein they reside. No State shall make or enforce any law which shall abridge the privileges or immunities of citizens of the United States; nor shall any State deprive any person of life, liberty, or property, without due process of law; nor deny to any person within its jurisdiction the equal protection of the laws.

The Fourteenth Amendment, in theory, provided equal status for African Americans. In practice, however, African Americans continued to endure racism and the deprivation of the rights which white citizens enjoyed. This has even included white immigrant groups who arrived in the United States after African Americans did. Although some European immigrant groups such as Italians and Irish did endure discrimination and prejudice in America, African Americans have been the group that has been consistently denied of their constitutional rights, to such an extent that it has required several amendments to the Constitution and the passage of civil right laws to protect the constitutional rights of African Americans; rights which are due to American citizens at birth.

Consider the fact that the Constitution itself had to be altered to provide more protections to African

Americans. The Constitution had to be amended just so that persons of African descent who were born free in the United States could be regarded as being equal with white citizens. Consider the numerous civil rights bills that were passed for the purpose of providing equal treatment and equal protection to African Americans. This is what Bobby E. Wright referred to when he stated that African Americans were a legally created people. It took the alteration of American law for African Americans to be regarded as equals under that very law. This created a separate legal status for African Americans, which was much different from the legal status of white citizens.

The struggle to obtain equal citizenship rights must also be understood in economic terms as well because the exploitation of African Americans was not merely a form of racial oppression, but a form of economic oppression as well; a type of oppression which benefited the financial interests of white citizens. African people were dragged to the United States for the purpose of being enslaved. African people did not willingly go to America to be worked as slaves. Moreover, slavery was an industry which many individuals profited from. Slaves were a commodity, which were bought and sold on auction blocks. The slave also worked for the slave master without pay.

The primary reason why Africans were brought to the United States was to be utilized for slave labor. For this reason, when the United States was founded, the laws which were implemented were laws which were consistent with America's slave society. The laws were also consistent with the white supremacist views held by some of the Founding Fathers. Thomas Jefferson, for example, expressed the view that "the blacks, whether originally a distinct race, or made distinct by time and circumstances, are inferior to the whites in the endowments both of body and mind."

The United States was not formed with the interests and the well-being of African people being a central focus. This was so painfully true that despite the horrible conditions which enslaved Africans had to endure inside of the slave ships which brought them to America, the Constitution ensured that the slave trade would be protected until 1801. Article 1, Section 9, Clause 1 reads: "The Migration or Importation of such Persons as any of the States now existing shall think proper to admit, shall not be prohibited by the Congress prior to the Year one thousand eight hundred and eight, but a Tax or duty may be imposed on such Importation, not exceeding ten dollars for each Person."

Newly liberated Africans were now making the transition away from being commodities in a slave society to being laborers in a capitalistic society. Slavery itself had played a significant role in the development of Western capitalism. This is a point that Eric Williams documented in his book *Capitalism and Slavery*. Unlike slaves, the worker in a capitalistic system is not owned by a master. In the system of capitalism, a worker freely contracts to provide his or her laborer to an employer who pays the worker a wage in return for the worker's labor. Whereas a slave is made to work against his or her will—often through the threat of force—the worker is compelled to work because the worker needs to earn a wage in order to pay for necessities such as food and shelter.

In the relationship between the employer and the employee, the employer generally maintains the dominant position. One does not have to adhere to Karl Marx's theories to understand that within the system of capitalism contradictions between the worker and the employer can and do arise. Marx envisioned that the working class would one day rebel against the capitalist ruling class and that this revolution would bring forward a communist society in which the means of production are commonly owned by the workers themselves rather than being owned and controlled by a few capitalists who profit from the labor of the working class.

America was never subjected to the type of communist inspired revolution which Russia experienced, but America certainly has not been immune to struggles between the working class and the owners of the means of production. The dangers of unrestrained capitalism are precisely why Marx envisioned an eventual uprising on the part of the working class, which would overturn the exploitative capitalist system. Such a revolution may very well have been inevitable in industrialized capitalist countries if not for reforms and regulations which restrict the power of the employer and provide protections for the employee. Far from overturning a system in which the working class labors for wages, the reforms ensure that the working class is not overworked and underpaid. These regulations have also ensured that children cannot be employed to work as laborers and that workers can be compensated if they are injured while working.

African people found themselves oppressed not only within a society that implemented a very strict racial hierarchy, but also a system with a class hierarchy as well. It is for this reason that civil rights legislation can be understood to be not only about protecting African Americans from racial discrimination, but also about protecting working people from being exploited by their employers. After all, an African who was denied a job on account of his or her race was not only being discriminated against racially but was also a victim of a capitalist system which places the worker at the mercy of the employer. Again, one does not need to adhere to the theories of Marx to understand that in an economic system where one's survival is based on the ability to earn a wage from an employer, there is an inherent inequality that can be easily exploited to the benefit of the employer and to the detriment of the employee.

The Supreme Court has often struggled with maintaining the balance between allowing capitalists to freely engage in the pursuit of enriching themselves and regulating businesses for the purpose of protecting the interests of workers. Where the two interests clashed, there were times when the Supreme Court took the side of the capitalist employer over that of the worker. This was very apparent during the so-called Lochner Era. This era is so called because of *Lochner v. New York*, 198 U.S. 45 (1905), which was a case in which the Supreme Court struck down a New York state law that regulated the working hours of bakers. *Lochner* was one of several cases in which the Supreme Court struck down measures that were implemented to improve the conditions of American workers.

In *Lochner*, Justice Rufus Peckham, who delivered the opinion, declared that the "general right to make a contract in relation to his business is part of the liberty of the individual protected by the Fourteenth

Amendment of the Federal Constitution." Justice Peckham continued to explain that the "right to purchase or to sell labor is part of the liberty protected by this amendment, unless there are circumstances which exclude the right." The Supreme Court in *Lochner* held that working hours for bakers was not one of those circumstances where the right to purchase and sell labor should be abridged. Justice Peckham explained: "There is no reasonable ground for interfering with the liberty of person or the right of free contract, by determining the hours of labor, in the occupation of a baker."

Justice Peckham cited *Holden v. Hardy*, 169 U.S. 366 (1989) which was a case in which the Supreme Court held that a law limiting the work hours of miners and smelters was a valid exercise of police power by the State, but Justice Peckham explained that the ruling in *Holden* did not apply in *Lochner*. Peckham explained that the law limiting the work hours of bakers was not related to protecting the safety of the bakers or the well-being of the public, as clean and wholesome "bread does not depend upon whether the baker works but ten hours per day or only sixty hours a week."

Peckham indicated that limiting the work hours of bakers was not as serious a concern as limiting the working hours of miners, but there was yet another issue that factored into the Supreme Court's ruling in *Lochner*. That issue was the power of the State versus the liberty of individuals. Justice Peckham explained as much when he framed the case as being "a question of which of two powers or rights shall prevail—the power of the State to legislate or the right of the individual to liberty of person and freedom of contract." In this case, the right of individual liberty and freedom of contract prevailed.

In *Lochner*, Peckham declared that "the liberty of contract relating to labor includes both parties to it. The one has as much right to purchase as the other to sell labor." The rights are not equal, however. In a capitalist economy, the party contracting for the purchase of labor typically has a number of advantages over the party contracting to sell his or her labor. A most obvious advantage is that the employee relies on the income he or she receives from the employer. For this reason, the employer is in a better position to dictate the terms of employment to the employee.

Yet another advantage which employers enjoy is the at-will doctrine, which allows an employer to discharge an employee for any reason at all. The Supreme Court of Alabama in *Allied Supply Co. v. Brown*, 585 So. 2d 33, 35 (Ala.1991) described the doctrine as thus: "Employees at will can terminate their employment, or can be terminated by their employer, at any time, with or without cause or justification." The Supreme Court of Alabama noted that the "at-will" doctrine has been criticized as being harsh, but that it remained the law in Alabama. The Supreme Court of Tennessee held in *Payne v. Western & Atlantic. R.R.*, 81 Tenn. (1884) that men "must be left, without interference to buy and sell where they please, and to discharge or retain employees at will for good cause or for no cause, or even for bad cause without thereby being guilty of an unlawful act per se."

The Supreme Court of Tennessee in *Payne* quoted Judge Cooley, who stated: "It is a part of every man's civil rights that he be at liberty to refuse business relations with any person whomsoever, whether the refusal rests upon reason, or is the result of whim, caprice, prejudice or malice. With his reasons neither the public nor third persons have any legal concern." The logic expressed by Cooley here is precisely the type of logic used to defend racial segregation. Under such reasoning, it would be the civil right of every man to deny business relations to an African American solely on the basis of prejudice and it would not be of any legal concern to the African American who is denied business relations.

Should racists be forced to contract with African Americans? Holding such a view necessarily entails that certain rights on the part of the racist individual will be curtailed or infringed upon. How far then can the law go to establish racial equality? How far should the law go? These are questions that must be asked in order to assess the role that legislation has played in attempting to resolve the problem of racial discrimination in the United States. Prior to the civil rights movement, courts adopted the view that the law must not go too far in imposing against the segregationist because doing so would infringe on one's freedom to reject engaging in business relations with whomever one pleases and for whatever reason one chooses.

There is also the question of whether or not it is practical for racial problems to be addressed through imposing racial integration against the will of the racists. The argument against this is not only that it infringes upon the rights of the racist, but that it would perhaps be better for African Americans to avoid being around racists who harbor such negative, bigoted, and hateful views. Perhaps it may be in the best interests of African Americans to avoid such racist individuals altogether. The problem with this approach is that racial separation in of itself is not a solution to the problem so long as rules which are designed to restrict the rights of African Americans remain in place.

As a minister of the Nation of Islam, Malcolm X drew a distinction between segregation and racial separation. In an interview with Eleanor Fischer, Malcolm X explained his views, stating: "Segregation is that which is forced upon an inferior by a superior. Separation is done voluntarily by two equals." Segregation was imposed upon African Americans. Segregation was the law and this law was implemented to enforce racial inequality.

What of separation? Malcolm X said that separation was done on a voluntary basis by two equals. The problem here is that there was an unequal relationship and for this reason African Americans were not free to build separately or independently from the dominant white society. The Nation of Islam preached a doctrine of racial separation. To achieve this vision of separation, Elijah Muhammad advocated the creation of a separate state for black people. The Nation of Islam was free to preach separation, but the Nation of Islam lacked the power or capacity to truly carry out this separation and the American government was certainly not going to give into the Nation of Islam's demands for land to build a separate nation. The Republic of New Afrika also demanded land to create a separate black nation.

Just as those who struggled for integration were met with a backlash, the Nation of Islam and other black separatist organizations were met with a similar backlash. Segregation was the law. Any attempts at racial integration were therefore a violation of that law, yet the segregationists did not view the black separatists as being preferable to the integrationists. On the contrary, black nationalism and the doctrine of black separation was viewed as a threat because it was an assertion of African American independence. The entire purpose of segregation was to keep African Americans in their place; to keep African Americans oppressed and subjugated. Integration was a threat to the status quo, but assertions of African American independence were also a threat as well because it was contrary to the goal of keeping African Americans subjugated.

Due to the threat of African American independence, building separate institutions from white people has been a challenge because when African Americans have done so it has been perceived as competing against white interests and eliminated for this reason. Ida B. Wells-Barnett was a well-known anti-lynching activist whose activism was motivated by the fact that her friend Thomas Moss had been lynched because Moss opened a grocery store, which was seen as a threat to a nearby white owned grocery store. African Americans did not have the freedom to patronize white owned businesses, but African Americans could not open and operate their own businesses without facing discrimination either. Therefore, separation alone is not a solution so long as African people do not have the necessary protection from white aggression.

The racialized nature of the United States created in a situation in which African Americans were both exploited for their labor while also being locked out of full participation within American capitalism. Even with the previously mentioned amendments, African Americans have continued to face racial discrimination where labor is concerned.

5 A NEW CLASS SYSTEM IN AFRICA

The Russian Revolution of 1917 was the historical event which popularized socialism as a revolutionary political force which challenged the exploitative nature of capitalism. Russia's revolution also helped to popularize Marxism, which is a historical and economic theory based on the writings of Karl Marx and Friedrich Engels. Marxism helped to influence and inspire revolutionary struggles around the world.

Marxism works as a method for historical analysis which can be used to understand the nature of the relationship between social organization and modes of production. Marxism also explains how changing modes of production create changes in a society's social organization. Marx documented these changes in Europe's history. He pointed out that Europe started with communalism. This was a stage in which property was collectively owned. This was followed by slavery in which slaves worked for their masters. This was then followed by feudalism. Unlike slaves, the feudal serfs were not the property of the master. The serf worked on land which belonged to a manor or estate. When the manor changed hands, the serfs remained and continued to work for the landlord. Finally, came capitalism in which machines generated the greatest wealth in society. Capitalism was also marked by greater freedom and social mobility for the laborers. Whereas slaves belonged to slave owners and serfs belonged to estates, workers in the capitalist system are free to pursue work for whomever will hire them. Of course, this freedom to seek work is still restricted by the fact that the bourgeoisie in the capitalist system retains ultimate control over a worker's destiny, but the worker in capitalism has more freedom than the slave and the serf had.

Yet another feature of capitalism is greater division of labor. Division of labor refers to the separation of tasks within the economic system. For example, a teacher performs the task of educating students. Teachers are individuals who specialize in providing education. This is a different task than a musician who specializes in making music and who serves the function of providing entertainment. This is also different from the factory worker who is trained to perform the task of working in a factory to produce goods. The task of the factory worker is different from the farmer who is trained in producing food.

Division of labor ensures the effective management of a given economy by ensuring that individuals are paid to perform the tasks which they are skilled at performing. These different tasks are necessary to sustain the economic system as a whole. For example, farmers produce food so that the factory worker does not need to worry about growing his own food. This creates specialization, which means that an individual professional can specialize as a worker in his or her field without having to worry about managing other aspects of the society.

The author Bryan Ward-Perkins explained that civilizations are very complex and that everyone relies on the comfort which this complexity gives us. He gave the example of sitting in a room with good heating and an internet connection. He noted that these things were basic to his existence and yet it takes a very complex social organization to sustain this. He also noted that hundreds of thousands of people are involved in sustaining this complex social organization. This network of specialization is what makes it possible for Ward-Perkins to sit in a heated room with an internet connection. I mention this to make the point that capitalism was more than a mere shift in production. The emergence of capitalism resulted in a complex form of social organization which can only be sustained by specialization and division of labor.

In Marx's view, capitalism was to follow the same fate as slavery and feudalism. Though capitalism provided greater freedoms for the laborer and provided technological advancements which improved quality of life, Marx believed that capitalism would eventually fall and that a new system would emerge. Marx envisioned that the working class would rise up and overthrow the capitalist ruling class to produce a new society. This new society would be a communist society in which the workers themselves had control over the means of production.

One of the limitations of Marxism where the African revolutionary struggle is concerned is that Africa's historical mode of development was not the same as Western Europe's. Marx. As was explained, Marx saw capitalism as a particular stage of Western Europe's historical development which would eventually be supplanted by another stage. For African people, capitalism was not a stage in our historical development, but a system which was imposed as part of the colonial process. We found ourselves being victims within a capitalist system which we did not create and which did not emerge out of our societies.

Even so, the relevance of Marxism within the Pan-African struggle was the fact that the introduction of capitalism via colonialism altered class structures and class relations in Africa such that these new classes which emerged did reflect what Marxists would refer to as the "petty bourgeoisie."

Whereas Mao believed that Cultural Revolution to wipe away China's traditional Confucian based culture was needed to build socialism in China, Kwame Ture did not view Africa's traditional culture as an obstacle which needed to be removed to establish socialism in Africa. He instead viewed Africa's culture as a tool to be utilized in the service of the revolutionary struggle. Ture embraced African culture as an aspect of Africa's revolutionary struggle. Ture argued that the values of socialism came from communalism. He further argued that communalism rested in Africa for a long period of time and that feudalism in Africa did not reach "the terroristic aspects" that it reached in other areas of the world.

The brutal nature of feudalism in Europe could be demonstrated by the peasant revolt of 1381. The peasant revolt of 1381 was one of the most significant events in English history because it represented a serious challenge to the existing political order. One of the causes for this revolt was the "Black Death" plague which had killed so many people that it created labour shortages in the country. A law known as the Statute of Labourers was implemented to keep wages for peasants at the same level that wages were at prior to the plague. This was combined with a new tax which was introduced.

Richard II was the king of England at the time and needed to pay for the costs of England's conflict with

France. The pressure was too much for the peasants and the peasants made their way to London to plead their case to the king. The peasants were led by a man named Wat Tyler. On the way to London, the peasants attacked several properties in England and executed those who were perceived as being hostile to the cause of the peasants. The peasants also freed the prisoners from London's jail.

Once the peasants made their way to London, their numbers grew. Their attacks also continued. They made their way to the Savoy Palace, destroying the palace room by room. The palace was then set on fire. The peasants moved throughout London, setting buildings on fire and executing their enemies.

The peasants made their way to the Tower of London. Richard II left the Tower to meet with the peasants. While the king was out, the Tower of London was stormed by hundreds of the rebel peasants. The peasants found the Archbishop of Canterbury Simon Sudbury and Robert Hales hiding in the tower. These two men and others were dragged out of the tower and beheaded. Their heads were paraded around the city.

The violence continued as the rebel peasants moved throughout the city, executing more enemies. Richard agreed to meet with the rebel leader, Wat Tyler. Tyler requested more changes to improve the lives of peasants. The meeting ended when William Walworth, the mayor of London, attacked Tyler. Tyler allegedly tried to lunge at the king. Walworth stabbed Tyler. Tyler was stabbed several more times by one of the king's servants. The encounter resulted in Tyler's death.

Surprisingly, Richard managed to calm the rebels

down. The murder of the rebel leader did not incite more violence on the part of the rebel peasants who had already caused great death and destruction throughout England. Tyler's head was placed on a spike and displayed. Richard II managed to successfully put down the revolt.

African societies tended to be more communal than feudal European societies were, though the extent to which communalism remained a dominant feature in Africa's social organization is debatable. In *African Voices of the Atlantic Trade*, Anne Bailey argued that communalism in Africa was not as dominant as Walter Rodney had claimed and that the veneer of communalism in some African societies did not take away from the underlying presence of different social relationships. Rodney himself had pointed to the existence of these different social relationships and wrote about the role that these different social relationships played in the slave trade, just as Anne Bailey did.

In his book *A History of the Upper Guinea Coast*, Rodney explained: "The responsibility for the slave trade, as far as Africans themselves bear part of this responsibility, lies squarely upon the shoulders of the tribal rulers and élites. They were in alliance with the European slave merchants and it was upon the mass of the people that they jointly preyed." He also explained: "The prevalent communal image of African society may serve to obscure the decisive differences between the masses and the nobility. It is true that a village chief might be related to most of the residents of the village, but even though for certain purposes he acted as family head, there remains little doubt that his level of subsistence was markedly superior to that of his poorer relations."

Amilcar Cabral addressed the pre-colonial class structure in Guinea-Bissau, which was not uniformly developed. The Balanta people developed what Cabral called "a horizontal society," which meant that there were no classes above another. There were no great chiefs until the Portuguese arrived and made chiefs for the Balanta people. Regarding the individual accumulation of wealth, Cabral stated: "Balanta society is like this: the more land you work, the richer you are, but the wealth is not to be hoarded, it is to be spent, for one individual cannot be much more than another."

Cabral explained that others had vertical societies, in which there was a chief at the top. The chiefs along with religious leaders formed what Cabral called a class. Then there were professionals such as clobbers, blacksmiths, and goldsmiths who did not have the same rights as those at the top. Cabral explained that by tradition, "anyone who was a goldsmith was even ashamed of it—all the more if he were a 'griot' (minstrel)."

Below the professionals there were those who tilled the ground. The tillers tilled the ground for the chiefs. Cabral explained that in Fula and Manjaco society, chiefs were linked to God and for this reason held authority over the tillers. Among the Majaco people, a tiller could not till without the chief's order.

Cabral noted that the nature of Fula society was structured to maintain this class hierarchy, but this is not to suggest that there were not conflicts. Cabral explained that there have been major peasant uprisings among the Fula people. In one instance, Mussa Molo overthrew a king and took the king's place. Cabral noted that this overthrow did not result in a significant structural change because Mussa Molo kept the same laws in place. Here we see an that class conflicts existed in pre-colonial Africa which were not unlike the previously mentioned 1381 uprising in England.

Cabral was forced to confront contradictions between ethnic groups, which were displayed not only in terms of different social structures among the various ethnic groups, but also in terms of prior military conflicts among the ethnic groups. Cabral explained that the Fula and Mandinga, unlike the Balanta, had chiefs. Cabral also explained that the majority of Fula and Mandinga in Guinea-Bissau were persons who became Mandinga and Fula. Cabral spoke of individuals being "Mandingized" as a result of Mandingo conquests.

The expansion of kingdoms resulted in wars and conquests in which certain conquered groups became absorbed into the dominant group. Wars and conflicts of this nature were an aspect of Africa's own internal development, but such conflicts were used by the Portuguese to provoke divisions among the people as part of the colonial divide and conquer tactic which kept Africans divided among each other thereby making it easier for Europeans to conquer and subjugate African people. Cabral sought to unite the society around chasing out the Portuguese colonizers.

Cabral also sought to unify the three classes in his society: the ruling class, the artisan class, and the peasant class. He recognized that this did not mean that everyone had to be united. In fact, Cabral acknowledged that there were certain self-interested individuals who "are afraid of losing their privileges in favour of the struggle."

In Thomas Sankara's view the roots of corruption in Burkina Faso came from the capitalist system, which is "a socioeconomic system that cannot really advance without developing corruption." Sankara also viewed corruption as "unquestionably a curse inherited from colonization." Sankara was, by his own admission, not "a well-informed sociologist, or a historian of precapitalist African societies," but he did not believe that the African rulers that were engaged in the slave trade for the purpose of acquiring items such as glass beads represented the same class of corrupt leadership which took control of post-colonial African nations. Sankara explained: "Regarding the feudal kings used by the colonizers, the handfuls of glass beads, from the African standpoint, were not the same as corruption to the extent that the mode of exchange was built on barter. The petty kings sold their "brothers" for one or another object of value that we consider in hindsight to be trinkets. […] A king who had never seen himself in a mirror would not hesitate to obtain it in exchange for a man, that is, for one of his subjects. Based on this fact, he is giving the corresponding value in exchange for this thing. He cannot be considered corrupt even if the colonizer or the explorer, given the economic system their society had attained, approached him on the basis of corruption."

The points raised by Rodney, Cabral, and Sankara demonstrate that there was a clear difference between the masses and the nobility in pre-colonial African states, but this relationship was not akin to the class relations which existed in European societies. Sankara's point is especially significant because he noted that even though African kings engaged in the slave trade—and as Rodney noted, it was primarily the elite in Africa who participated in and benefitted from the slave trade—these rulers viewed the trade as a legitimate form of barter and not as a form of corruption which he explained was brough into Burkina Faso via colonialism and capitalism.

It is also important to note that even though the African elite did participate in the slave trade, the trade itself was largely controlled by Europeans. King Affonso I of the Kongo Kingdom tried to establish ties with the Portuguese. He willingly converted to Christianity and learned how to read and write in Portuguese—one of the priests wrote that Affonso knew the prophets and the Gospel better than they did. He also expressed a desire for the Portuguese to send priests, doctors, and other specialists because he eagerly wanted his people to learn from the Portuguese. Instead, the Portuguese sent slavers to acquire more slaves. Affonso was initially involved in the slave trade. He sold his captives as slaves, but the Portuguese greed for slaves became too overwhelming. The Portuguese began kidnapping and enslaving free Africans. Affonso wrote a series of letters to the Portuguese king (King Joao II) pleading to stop the practice of stealing freed subjects and enslaving them.

Affonso wrote: "Each day the traders are kidnapping our people—children of this country, sons of our nobles and vassals, even people of our own family…This corruption and depravity are so widespread that our land is entirely depopulated…" Affonso further writes: "It is our wish that this kingdom not be a place for the trade or transport of slaves."

Affonso also noted that the greed of his people drove them to seize members of their own families and sell them into slavery. The slave trade had gotten out of the control of King Affonso and he desperately wanted an end to it. The Portuguese paid little attention to Affonso's request and continued their trade of African slaves, however. In 1539 King Affonso found out that 10 of his relatives, including nephews and grandchildren, had disappeared en route to Portugal. They would become slaves in Brazil. Affonso's opposition to the slave trade did not go over well with some of the Portuguese traders. In 1540 some Portuguese merchants made an attempt to assassinate King Affonso, but it failed.

Dahomey offers another example. . King Agaja Trudo, who reigned in the 1700s, recognized that the European demand for slaves was harmful to Dahomey's development. He responded to this by attacking and burning European forts along the coast. He also attacked trade factories in Allada and Whydah. Agaja had his troops block the paths that led into the interior, which greatly reduced the number of slaves being exported.

The Europeans were unable to defeat Agaja, but Agaja was also unsuccessful in his attempt to pursue other means of business with the Europeans. He sent a spokesman to England to appeal to European craftsmen. One European who stayed at the court of Dahomey in the 1720s stated "if any tailor, carpenter, smith or any other sort of white man that is free be willing to come here, he will find very good encouragement." Agaja found no success in this, however, as the only means of business which the

Europeans wished to pursue was slave trading. Agaja's need for guns forced him to reach an agreement with the Europeans.

The case of the Olympio family in Togo further illustrates the fact that although some Africans participated in and benefitted from the slave trade, the trade itself was firmly controlled by the European elite. The Olympio family in Togo is one which traces its roots to Brazil. Francisco Olympio Silva was born in Brazil on July 24, 1833. His mother was African and Amerindian. Francisco moved to Togo in 1850 at the age of 17. He was among the many Brazilians who relocated to Togo. In Africa, Francisco became involved in the slave trade. When the slave trade was ended in 1865, Francisco was forced to turn to other business ventures. He became a planter and commercial trader. Francisco likely employed slaves who would have been exported to Brazil to work as laborers on his plantations. At some point, Francisco dropped the name Silva. He also established a large family. He had seven wives and twenty-one children.

The African slave trader operated as an agent within the system. Within this system the slave trader held relatively little power in comparison to the Europeans who controlled and operated the system. They were willful participants to the extent that the slave trade did benefit them individually, but most of the wealth generated from the trade was held in the hands of the Europeans who controlled the trade. Europeans also controlled the terms of the trade.

The same situation existed during colonialism and after. One by one, kingdoms in Africa fell to the colonial powers. The colonial powers in turn created a new political system which stripped power from the traditional rulers and placed them in the hands of an emerging political elite which the colonizers produced. This was the genesis of the neo-colonial elite. Ngũgĩ wa Thiong'o explained: "It is true that the African middle class, which led the faction committed to anticolonial nationalism, wanted freedom from colonial laws, racial barriers, and a racialized view of the world that put whiteness at the center and denied the class movement. But this nationalist class, critiqued by Frantz Fanon in terms of pitfalls of national consciousness in his book *The Wretched of the Earth*, did not come into leadership of the new states as an independent bourgeoisie: It was soon ensnared in neocolonialism, cold-war politics, and globalization."

Colonialism not only introduced the capitalist system in Africa, but it also changed class relations so that the class which emerged in the post-colonial period was a middle class which was connected to the colonial capitalist system both culturally and financially. Leon M'ba, who was the president of Gabon, was known to have said that all Gabonese have two fatherlands, Gabon and France. We are so colonized that we cannot tell ourselves apart from the people that have colonized us, and as a result we think that their interests are our interests when the reality is that they have a vested interest in our continued oppression and colonization. A *New York Times* report from 1964 described M'ba, who had recently been overthrown, as "one of France's best friends in Africa." ("Man in the News; Ousted Gabonese," *New York Times*, Feb. 19, 1964). That's how closely connected to colonialism these leaders were culturally. There was an economic connection as well.

In *Africa Must Unite*, Kwame Nkrumah wrote that a number of political demonstrations and strikes took place throughout Africa prior to World War II. During the 1940s, many organizations were formed, such as the National Council of Nigeria and the Cameroons, as well as the Nyasaland National Congress. In the Gold Coast, Nkrumah formed the Convention People's Party. Nkrumah noted that these parties acted as unifying forces in Africa. In Nkrumah's view, the C.P.P. represented the ordinary, common folk of Ghana. He contrasted this with the opposition party which was supported by lawyers and other conservative professionals who did not understand the new mood of the people.

Nkrumah had previously served as secretary of the United Gold Coast Convention (U.G.C.C.). Nkrumah stated that the leaders of the U.G.C.C. were frightened to learn that Nkrumah had spearheaded a mass movement. He explained: "They had wanted me to build up a movement whose ranks would not question their self-assumed right to political leadership, but would nevertheless provide a solid enough base for them to pose as the national champions in pressing for constitutional change. It was when the leaders of the U.G.C.C. demanded I get rid of the mass following I had built up, that I withdrew from their secretariat, and formed the Convention People's Party."

Nkrumah was describing a conflict which would become more pronounced in the post-colonial period. During colonialism, there arose a class within the African population which managed to carve out a comfortable living for themselves as professionals within the colonial system. This was the class which seized power following the formal end of colonialism.

This new neo-colonial class continues to enjoy a degree of comfort as the African masses continue to struggle.

The roots of this neo-colonial class can be traced to the development of colonialism in Africa. There were various Africans who aligned with and supported colonialism for one reason or another. Bishop Samuel Ajayi Crowther in Nigeria, for example, defended colonialism because it brought Christianity to Africa. This is an example of the fact that some Africans embraced colonialism. The nationalist leaders in Africa were generally opposed to colonialism, although many of these nationalist leaders were themselves highly influenced by colonialism. The result was that these leaders opposed colonialism, but also kept the colonial system in place once in power. These anti-colonial leaders would prove themselves to be little more than opportunists who fought colonialism so that they could replace the colonizers as exploiters of the African masses.

In Ghana, Nkrumah sought to pursue a path of socialist development to guarantee full employment, good housing, equal educational opportunity, and cultural advancement for all. Nkrumah believed that the government had to "play the role of main entrepreneur in laying the basis of the national economic and social advancement." In Nkrumah's view, to turn the country over to private interests would be an act of "betraying the trust of the great masses of our people for the greedy interests of a small coterie of individuals, probably in alliance with foreign capitalist." It was indeed foreign capitalists who overthrew Nkrumah in a coup. The United States and other Western powers would not tolerate any attempt to transform Africa through socialism, especially in the 1960s as the United States was waging its ideological struggle with the Soviet Union. For the United States, winning the Cold War and retaining control in Africa meant ensuring that the neo-colonial class remained firmly in power. In doing so, American capitalism helped to firmly entrench the neo-colonial class in Africa, thereby completing the process of altering class relations in African society. This was a process which began during the slave trade and continued during colonialism.

6 KWAME TURE VERSUS THE BLACK PANTHERS

Differing views on ideology also led to a split between the Black Panther Party and Stokely Carmichael, the former chairman of the Student Non-Violent Coordinating Committee (SNCC). Unlike Carmichael, the Panthers were open to working with white people, which became a source of dispute when Carmichael urged the Panthers to cut their ties with whites. This caused Bobby Seale to denounce Carmichael. James Forman, who was also a member of SNCC along with Carmichael, sided with the Panthers in the split. Forman had grown uneasy with Carmichael's "reactionary nationalism" and decided to embrace Marxism instead.

Marxism-Leninism formed the basis of the Black Panther Party's ideology. This is why the study of Marxism-Leninism was compulsory among the learning cadre. Newton expressed that the socialist direction of the Black Panther Party was a clear break with the tradition of Marcus Garvey and Elijah Muhammad, stating: "The Black Panther Party grew out of the Black Power movement, but the Party transformed the ideology of Black Power into a socialist ideology, a Marxist-Leninist ideology. The Black Power movement has a tendency to have a capitalistic orientation along the lines of Marcus Garvey's program and the kind of organization that Elijah Muhammed has. The Black Panther Party feels that not even the Black bourgeoisie will be able to compete with imperialism, whose central base is here in North America."

Huey Newton's particular vision of Black Power also led to a break with Stokely Carmichael (later known as Kwame Ture) who had popularized Black Power. In a 1970 press conference, Newton charged that Carmichael was operating as an agent of the CIA, although Newton admitted that the Black Panthers had no proof of this. Newton did state that he had some evidence, however. This included Carmichael's public statement accusing the Black Panther Party of being dishonest. Newton also claimed that Carmichael's wife Miriam Makeba was an agent as well.

Newton also rejected Pan-Africanism. Whereas Carmichael believed that Pan-Africanism was the highest expression of Black Power, Newton dismissed Pan-Africanism as "the highest expression of cultural nationalism." He further stated that most African governments which adhere to Pan-Africanism are aligned with American imperialism. In Newton's view, Carmichael's philosophy was no different than the philosophy of reactionary governments in Africa. Newton made it clear that he supported Africa's struggle against imperialism, but he did not adhere to the philosophy of Pan-Africanism.

The remarks which Newton made demonstrated how much the relationship between the two men had become a contentious one. In 1967, Newton was referring to Carmichael as "Brother Stokely Carmichael". He also stated that because Carmichael had proven himself to be a true revolutionary who was guided by love for the people, Carmichael was drafted into the Black Panther Party to become a Field Marshal. The alliance between Carmichael and Newton ultimately failed due to ideological differences, but those differences became so serious that Newton began to openly accuse Carmichael of being an agent.

Carmichael, who later changed his name to Kwame Ture, left the Panthers and moved to Guinea in 1969 with his wife, the South African musician Miriam Makeba. Ture also aligned himself with Sékou Touré, who was the president of Guinea. In Guinea, Carmichael also met and worked with Kwame Nkrumah. Carmichel changed his name to Kwame Ture to honor both men. He also embraced the ideology of Nkrumahism-Toureism.

Ture expressed admiration for Marx and Lenin, but he could not embrace Marxism-Leninism because it was not rooted in Africa's culture. The Black Panther Party seemed to have recognized this as well, but rather than reject Marxism-Leninism as an ideology, the Panthers attempted to adopt the ideology to the realities of the African American struggle.

In a document titled "On the Ideology of the Black Panther Party," Eldridge Cleaver elaborated on the ideology of the Black Panther Party. He explained that the Black Panther Party viewed the struggle of black people in America through the prism of

Marxism-Leninism. The Panther's embrace of Marxism-Leninism was inspired largely by Frantz Fanon. In Cleaver's view, Fanon was the first major Marxist-Leninist theoretician "who was primarily concerned about Black people, wherever they may be found." Cleaver added that Fanon was primarily focused on Africa and that it "is only indirectly that his works are beneficial to Afro-Americans." Cleaver also noted that "Fanon delivered a devastating attack upon Marxism-Leninism for its narrow preoccupation with Europe and the affairs and salvation of White folks, while lumping all third world peoples into the category of the Lumpenproletariat and then forgetting them there; Fanon unearthed the category of the Lumpenproletariat and began to deal with it, recognizing that vast majorities of the colonized people fall into that category."

Cleaver acknowledged that Marxism has not dealt with the United States of America, though some attempts were made. Cleaver also noted that on "the subject of racism, Marxism-Leninism offers us very little assistance." He points out that evidence suggests that Marx himself was a racist, but he also expressed the view that the founding of the Democratic People's Republic of Korea and the People's Republic of China injected something new into Marxism-Leninism. Kim Il Sung and Mao applied the principles of Marxism-Leninism to their conditions and made the ideology of Marxism-Leninism useful to their people. The struggles in Korea and China demonstrated to the Black Panther Party that the ideology of Marxism-Leninism could be applied to the struggles of non-white people.

The challenge which the Black Panther Party

confronted was how to take an ideology which developed in Europe and apply it to the struggle of black people in the United States. The revolutionary struggle led by Mao in China and Kim Il Sung in Korea demonstrated to the Black Panther Party that Marxism-Leninism as an ideology could be applied to the revolutionary struggles of non-European people. Fanon also demonstrated to the Black Panther Party that Marxism-Leninism could be applied to the struggles of black people.

The Black Panther Party adopted Marxism-Leninism, but also applied the Marxist-Leninist ideology to their situation as an oppressed people—Cleaver argued that black people in America are a colonized people—in America. This also meant understanding that American capitalism was something different than the capitalist system which Marx had written about. Cleaver explained: "The Working Class that we must deal with today shows little resemblance to the Working Class of Marx's day. In the days of its infancy, insecurity, and instability, the Working Class was very revolutionary and carried forward the struggle against the bourgeoisie. But through long and bitter struggles, the Working Class has made some inroads into the Capitalist system, carving out a comfortable niche for itself." Cleaver noted that labor unions, collective bargaining, the Union Shop, and social security all played a role in transforming the working class into a "bought-off" labor movement that is only interested in higher wages and more job security. He denounced A. Phillip Randolph as a traitor to the proletariat, but he acknowledged that Randolph represented the aspirations of the working class in America because the American working class looked to the Democratic Party for its salvation.

Yet another area where the Panthers differed with Marx is on the role of the lumpenproletariat. Cleaver challenged the view that the lumpenproletariat was a parasite upon the working class. He argued that it was actually the American working class which was a parasite to the lumpenproletariat.

The approach which the Panthers engaged in was not one which pleased all Marxists. Henry Winston was especially critical of the Black Panthers. One of Winston's criticisms of the Black Panther Party was its rejection of non-violence. Winston writes: "When Newton advocated guns and a defensive Strategy as the solution for Black people, he was wrong on both counts. Not only did the people refuse to relate to the gun, but they also rejected the concept of a defensive strategy." Here Winston does make a rather sound argument. Newton himself had criticized Cleaver's approach, which he explained left the community no alternative but to pick up the gun.

Winston is also correct to state: "The pseudo-militancy of Newton, Cleaver and Hilliard made their own party and its supporters particularly vulnerable to nation-wide genocidal assaults and frameups." This is a point which I have been critical of as well. The approach of the Black Panther Party made them easy targets for frameups because their own violent rhetoric was often used against them in court.

Winston also criticizes the view held by the Black Panther Party that the lumpenproletariat is the vanguard of the revolution. This view obviously challenges established Marxist orthodoxy. After all, the *Communist Manifesto* stated that "the proletariat alone is a really revolutionary class." The Black Panthers disagreed and held the view that there was revolutionary potential among the lumpen. Winston also points out that the Black Panthers rely on Frantz Fanon to support their views, even though Fanon himself had reservations about the lumpen. Fanon wrote: "In Algeria it is the lumpenproletariat which furnished the harkis and the messalists; in Angola it supplied the road openers who now precede the Portuguese armed columns; in the Congo, we find once more the lumpenproletariat in regional manifestations in Katai and Katanga, while at Leopoldville, the Congo enemies made use of it to organize spontaneous mass meetings against Lumumba."

Winston's criticism of the Black Panther Party could largely be seen as a criticism of the Black Panthers for straying away from Marxist-Leninist orthodoxy. Part of the problem with the Black Panther Party was that the party struggled to establish a clear ideology. Winston quotes Newton who wrote that "the Black Panther party took a counter-revolutionary position with our blanket condemnation of Black capitalism." Winston accuses Newton of trying to gain access to white capital, which is why Newton changed his position on capitalism. He also accuses Newton of belonging to a group of "ultra-revolutionaries" who engaged in rhetoric which offered no solutions for black people. Bobby Seale wrote that Ron Karenga "had no intention before and has no intention now of working in opposition to the power structure to change the system for the needs of Black America." Winston charges that this statement was also applicable to Newton.

Ture faced contradictions of his own. Touré, an avowed socialist, eventually reconciled with the Western capitalistic nations in his later years. In 1982, Touré visited New York to encourage Western businessmen to invest in Guinea. Touré had denounced Felix Houphouët-Boigny of the Ivory Coast as being a neo-colonialist, but the year before Touré's death Houphouët-Boigny described Touré as a close friend and he touted Guinea as an example of the pro-Western approach towards economic and political development in Africa. When Touré died in 1984 he received various tributes from Western leaders and their African allies who defended their relationship with Touré. The *New York Times* reported: "He had been mellowing, Western diplomats and African conservatives said. He was no longer resorting to violent oppression as easily or often as he had in the past, they asserted."

Kwame Ture joined Western governments in defending Touré's government following Touré's death. Ture asserted that in "all the world's great historical movements from Christ's to Gandhi's, blood has had to flow." Political prisoners in Guinea were locked away at Camp Boiro where they endured horrific treatment such as being starved to death, being subjected to electric shock, being suspended over fire, and having their fingers broken. This was not enough for Kwame Ture, who felt that Touré was "too soft." Kwame Ture moved to Africa and adopted an African name, but Ture's continued support for Touré even after Touré adopted a pro-Western position demonstrates that Ture's embrace of Pan-Africanism was hindered by reactionary nationalist sentiments, which was precisely what Huey Newton was criticizing when he denounced cultural nationalism. In 1983, the *Workers Vanguard* accused Kwame Ture of embodying "reactionary utopian Pan-Africanism." This assessment is not entirely inaccurate given that Kwame Ture's embrace of Pan-Africanism ultimately resulted in embracing what was to become yet another Western supported African dictatorship.

Notes:

Clifford May, "Guinea's President, Sekou Toure, Dies in Cleveland Clinic," *New York Times*, March 28, 1984.

___ "In Post-Coup Guinea, A Jail Is Thrown Open," *New York Times*, April 12, 1984.

Henry Winston, *Strategy for a Black Agenda; a critique of new theories of liberation in the United States and Africa*, 1973.

Huey Newton, *To Die For the People: The Writings of Huey P. Newton*, 1972.

"SNCC: 'Black Power' and the Democrats," *Workers Vanguard*, April 8, 1983.

"The Rise and Fall of the Black Panther Party: A Revolutionary Marxist Analysis," *Workers Vanguard*, May 21, 1993.

7 THE LIMITATIONS OF MARXISM-LENINISM IN AFRICA

During the Cold War, some African states embraced Marxism-Leninism. It would seem that this embrace of Marxism-Leninism was rooted in the nature of Cold War politics, rather than rooted in a real desire to develop a working class society. I state this due to the manner in which many of the states which promoted Marxism-Leninism dropped the ideology when it became apparent that the Cold War was ending and the Soviets had lost.

In Mozambique, the Mozambique Liberation Front (Frente de Libertação de Moçambique or FRELIMO) established a one-party state and adopted the ideology of Marxism-Leninism. It is difficult to judge the true success of the Mozambique Liberation Front in the period following independence because Mozambique received its independence in 1975, and by 1977 a civil war broke out between the ruling government and the Mozambican National Resistance, which was an anti-communist organization that was supported by Rhodesia and South Africa. This war lasted until 1992 and what I want to note here is that before the war had finished, the Mozambique Liberation Front had abandoned communism. Joaquim Chissano took over control of the party when Samora Machel died, but he abandoned the ideology of Marxism-Leninism when it was becoming clear that the Soviet Union was losing the Cold War.

FRELIMO was formed in Tanzania in 1962 as an alliance of exiled political groups and began its armed struggle against Portuguese colonialism in 1964. There were internal struggles within the party itself. These struggles were often violent and led to the assassination of Eduardo Mondlane, who was the first president. His successor was Samora Machel, who stands out as being one of the most prominent African revolutionaries during this period of anti-colonial struggle in Africa. Under Machel's leadership, FRELIMO became a Marxist-Leninist organization. FRELIMO was also significantly influenced by China's experiences and by the ideas of Mao.

FRELIMO managed to defeat Portuguese colonialism and declare its independence. Under Machel's leadership, FRELIMO became a Marxist-Leninist political party. The discipline and integrity of Mozambique that was established under this new political direction is to be commended. Few party and government officials used their position to enrich themselves. Those who did were dismissed and occasionally executed. Mozambique had one of the lowest levels of corruption in Africa. I mention this to demonstrate that there were positive advances made by FRELIMO which should be recognized.

FRELIMO did face challenges, however. Independence was followed by 200,000 whites fleeing the country. This was a significant loss of skilled manpower, but Machel was undaunted in his attempt to transform Mozambique through nationalized plantations and businesses. Consistent with its Marxist-Leninist views, FRELIMO sought to reduce the influence of the Catholic Church by ordering an end to public religious festivals and taking over church property. This hostility extended to traditional religions as well. In 1977, Machel declared: "We affirm that our aim is to win total independence, to establish people's power, to build a new society without exploitation for the benefit of all those who consider themselves Mozambican."

Machel established himself as a respected revolutionary leader in Africa. After Machel died, Thomas Sankara described Machel as "a great friend of our revolution, a greater backer of our revolution." Indeed, the death of Machel was not only a blow to Mozambique, but a blow to the revolutionary struggle in Africa. Yet, there were already signs that socialism was weakening in Mozambique, even under Machel's leadership.

The government's policies failed to resolve the economic challenges that the nation was facing. FRELIMO debated whether to allow the peasantry to take back control of the land or to preserve the colonial infrastructure. FRELIMO opted for the latter and set up a state farm sector. The peasantry was also forced into collective villages, in a policy that was similar to a policy pursued by Julius Nyerere in Tanzania. These policies were not only an economic failure, but it alienated FRELIMO from much of the peasantry.

In "The Collapse of Mozambique Socialism," Dan

O'Meara explains that in the 1980s the government of Mozambique was in a "contradictory process" and that "the major trend was towards increasing control and freezing out of large-scale (or indeed any form of) democratic participation both in economic decision-making and in the political life of the country." FRELIMO laid out a ten-year plan which projected a targeted annual economic growth rate of 14.7%. This rate was to be achieved through maximizing exports, which meant maximizing the agricultural production of the peasantry. President Machel declared that this objective was achievable because Mozambique had a vanguard party, but this goal was not achieved. Huge development projects brought Mozambique into debt to capitalist economies. This debt was more than double Mozambique's pre-independence Gross Domestic Product.

There were also political issues within FRELIMO itself as well. O'Meara explained: "During these years FRELIMO was a highly contradictory political movement. On the one hand, it was extremely centralized and commandist, moving slowly towards a growing personality cult around Samora Machel. On the other hand, it was at that stage still highly responsive to all kinds of mass pressures, and indeed organised wide-ranging consultative processes at all levels of society."

Aside from the economic struggles, Mozambique also faced destabilization attempts as well—not unlike the destabilization attempts that Angola faced with the South African and American supported UNITA rebel group. The Mozambican National Resistance (Resistência Nacional Moçambicana or RENAMO) was a rebel group which was supported by Rhodesia and South Africa for the purpose of overthrowing FRELIMO in Mozambique. The conflict between FRELIMO and RENAMO was a very destructive one. Not only did it drain the nation's economy, but RENAMO also directed its attacks against the civilian population.

In 1984, Mozambique signed a pact with South Africa, known as the Nkomati Accord. The war had such a devastating impact on Mozambique that FRELIMO had little option but to try to negotiate peace with South Africa. The accord was in a sense a compromise with FRELIMO's prior revolutionary position, but the pact with South Africa was not treated as such. O'Meara explained: "The incredulous party members and *cooperantes* who could not quite make this leap were bluntly told that anybody who said otherwise was an imperialist agent, a Trotskyist counter-revolutionary, a petty bourgeois defeatist and a myriad [of] other nasty things that no-one wanted to be. This was the first time such language was used in Mozambique and it sapped what was left of the critical spirit in the party and amongst the intelligentsia. It also destroyed what was left of the political credibility of FRELIMO."

Not only did the Nkomati Accord weaken FRELIMO ideologically and politically, but it did not even achieve what Mozambique had hoped. This compromise with South Africa followed with 800 ANC members being expelled from Mozambique. Meanwhile, South Africa secretly continued its support of RENAMO. The war was so devastating and destructive that over one million Mozambicans were killed by violence or starvation.

There were a lot of challenges confronting

FRELIMO, but in the end the party opted to abandon Marxism-Leninism as the Cold War was coming to an end. Mengistu Haile Mariam of Ethiopia, José Eduardo dos Santos of Angola, Mathieu Kérékou of Benin, and Robert Mugabe of Zimbabwe also abandoned Marxism-Leninism at the end of the Cold War.

Mugabe offers a very curious example. To understand Robert Mugabe and the situation in Zimbabwe it is necessary to give some background information on the struggles against white minority rule in Zimbabwe. Mugabe emerged as a freedom fighter in opposition to the white minority ruled government in Rhodesia. The growing resistance towards white domination in Rhodesia had helped the Rhodesian Front political party to win a sweeping victory in 1962. In 1964, Ian Smith became the Prime Minister of Rhodesia after his predecessor Winston Field was removed.

One of the goals of the Rhodesian Front was to achieve independence from Britain, since Britain was seen as having abandoned the whites in their other colonies to be ruled by Africans. Smith's position was that either white people in Rhodesia had to declare their independence or face the prospect of African rule. In 1965, Smith decided to unilaterally declare Rhodesia's independence from Britain. The Proclamation of Independence that was written resembled the American Declaration of Independence in 1776. Smith declared, "We have struck a blow for the preservation of justice, civilisation and Christianity." Rhodesia's independence was not recognized internationally, however. Rhodesia's independence would not be recognized until 1980, when, in the newly renamed Zimbabwe, Robert Mugabe was elected as the Prime Minister.

Despite his eventual strained relations with the West, Mugabe initially came to power with American and British support. Mugabe initially pursued a policy of reconciliation with whites. This included appointing two white ministers in his cabinet and retaining the former Rhodesian armed commander General Peter Walls as Zimbabwe's military chief. Mugabe even maintained good relations with Ian Smith.

During the first year of independence Zimbabwe received almost 900 million pounds in Western aid, which was used to finance a number of programs, including a land resettlement program. To protect the land rights of the white settlers, there was an agreement which stipulated that land transactions could only be conducted by a willing-seller. This was meant to reassure whites about their land rights. Mugabe's policies were clearly meant to ease the concerns that whites had over African majority rule, but Mugabe's policies were ruthless when it came to African political rivals. Mugabe's stated goal was to establish a one-party state.

Joshua Nkomo, who was once an ally of Mugabe's, was soon to become one of the many political victims of Mugabe's rule. Nkomo founded and led the Zimbabwe African People's Union (ZAPU) of which Mugabe was once a part of, but Nkomo's influence began waning within the organization. Eventually a number of followers of ZAPU broke away and formed the Zimbabwe African National Union (ZANU) in 1963. Much of the motivation for the split was the less militant approach that Nkomo had towards the struggle. In December 1974, Mugabe and Nkomo were released after being in detention camp since August 1964 following Smith's decision to ban both ZANU and ZAPU, and to jail the leaders of both organizations. Following their release, Nkomo was willing to engage in negotiation with Ian Smith, but Mugabe rejected this idea. For Mugabe liberation could only be achieved through armed struggle. As Mugabe continued to wage this struggle, Smith was engaged in a series of negotiations with Nkomo, which began in December 1975. These negotiations made little progress, and Smith himself affirmed, "I don't believe in majority rule, black majority rule, ever in Rhodesia, not in a thousand years."

In 1980 it was ZANU that won the elections and it was Mugabe who became the nation's first Prime Minister. Mugabe and Nkomo had once been allies in the struggle against white minority rule, but in the newly independent Zimbabwe, ZAPU and ZANU were fierce political rivals—although prior to independence the rivalry between ZANU and ZAPU became at times a violent one. For Mugabe, ZAPU was simply an obstacle in the way of his goal to create a one-party state in Zimbabwe.

The differences between the two parties became particularly destructive when Mugabe sent his Five Brigade to hunt down those who were loyal to Nkomo. This resulted in the deaths of thousands of Zimbabweans. Nkomo himself was forced to flee to Botswana and then to London after his home was attacked and his driver was killed. Nkomo was appointed as the Home Affairs Minister in Mugabe's government, but had been dismissed in 1982 after being accused of plotting a coup.

Throughout his presidency, Mugabe has overseen the collapse of Zimbabwe's economy and a number of political scandals relating to corruption within the ruling party. After a decade of independence the average Zimbabwean citizen struggled to find employment, but Zimbabwean ministers grew wealthy. The land resettlement program was also moving slowly and that too benefited politicians more than it did the average Zimbabwean. In 1994, it was discovered by a newspaper that a 3,000 acre farm that the government had purchased against the will of the white owner was leased to a government minister named Witness Mangwende. This was followed by an investigation which exposed that about 300 farms that were meant for resettlement had gone to government ministers and officials instead. By the 1990s Zimbabwe was in a state of economic crisis and the infrastructure in the nation was crumbling. Despite this, Mugabe involved Zimbabwe in a costly war in the Congo in 1998. The war, which was estimated to cost $1 million a day, put Zimbabwe in further debt.

Obviously, such a situation was contrary to the type of workers state which a Marxist-Leninist is supposed to be trying to build, but Mugabe himself acknowledged that his party was never truly Marxist in practice. In an interview with *HARDtalk*, Mugabe explained that his political party eventually shed some of its Marxist ideology. He admitted, "we were more Marxist in theory than we were in practice." That Mugabe himself admitted that he shifted away from Marxism is fascinating because it demonstrates that Mugabe spent the 1980s pursuing an ideology which he would later turn away from, demonstrating that a single leader or single political party does not always contain the answers to a nation's problems. The problem is that in many Marxist-Leninist states during this period, the development of one-party states meant that those with the foresight to see that certain policies were not working were often silenced for daring to voice these criticisms. In other words, the voice of the masses was silenced in the name of developing one-party rule.

I don't think that many of the African political leaders that embraced Marxism were really trying to build a true communist society. What many of them were really doing was copying the Soviet model, which was a one-party state ruled by what was supposed to be a vanguard party. They were not truly working to create a state where workers were not being exploited and where there was common ownership of the means of production. Their ideological attachment was not to Marxism itself, but to the Soviet Union and when the Soviet Union fell, these political leaders had no choice but to adopt a new line of thinking.